Liquid Evil
Living with TINA

Zygmunt Bauman &
Leonidas Donskis

polity

The right of Zygmunt Bauman and Leonidas Donskis to be identified as Authors of this Work has been asserted in accordance with the UK Copyright, Designs and Patents Act 1988.

First published in 2016 by Polity Press

Polity Press
65 Bridge Street
Cambridge CB2 1UR, UK

Polity Press
350 Main Street
Malden, MA 02148, USA

ISBN-13: 978-1-5095-0811-2
ISBN-13: 978-1-5095-0812-9 (pb)

A catalogue record for this book is available from the British Library.

Library of Congress Cataloging-in-Publication Data

Bauman, Zygmunt, 1925-
    Liquid evil / Zygmunt Bauman, Leonidas Donskis.
        pages cm
    Includes bibliographical references and index.
    ISBN 978-1-5095-0811-2 (hardback) – ISBN 978-1-5095-0812-9 (pbk.)   1. Good and evil.   I. Title.
    BJ1401.B38 2015
    170–dc23
                                                                            2015024822

Typeset in 11 on 13 pt Sabon
by Toppan Best-set Premedia Limited
Printed and bound by CPI Group (UK) Ltd, Croydon, CR0 4YY.

The publisher has used its best endeavours to ensure that the URLs for external websites referred to in this book are correct and active at the time of going to press. However, the publisher has no responsibility for the websites and can make no guarantee that a site will remain live or that the content is or will remain appropriate.

Every effort has been made to trace all copyright holders, but if any have been inadvertently overlooked the publisher will be pleased to include any necessary credits in any subsequent reprint or edition.

For further information on Polity, visit our website:
politybooks.com

Contents

About This Book

But a few days after putting the finishing touches to the transcript of our conversation (published two years ago by Polity under the title *Moral Blindness*), we realized that our conversation needed to continue. Too many strings attached remained untied, and too many new ones, first invisible but by then increasingly salient, demanded to be put on record and tried to be tied. This was not the fault of authors stopping their analytical efforts prematurely, before the task had reached its completion – but the consequence of the very nature of the undertaking.

While evil as such – the object of our investigation – can be seen as a permanent, inalienable companion of the human condition, its forms and ways of operation, particularly in their present-day liquidized incarnation, are novel phenomena; they deserve separate treatment, in which precisely their novelty is cast in the centre of attention. It is in the nature of all liquids that they are incapable of keeping any of their successively adopted shapes and forms for long. Liquids are perpetually *in statu nascendi* – always 'becoming', rather than having acquired an accomplished form: a quality noted more than two millennia ago by Heraclitus, observing that one can't step twice into the same river, as noted by Plato in his *Cratylus* dialogue. What one can – and needs to – do, when aiming at its fullest possible representation, is to discover the river's sources and its most copious tributaries, trace the trajectory of the riverbed (or, if such needs arise, its multiple – coexisting or alternating – trajectories), and map them both (even if being aware that what can ultimately be achieved is more of the nature of a snapshot than of the conclusive, lasting image of the phenomenon in question).

This is exactly what we try to do in this book: to chart as fully as possible the currently most prolific sources of evil, and follow as many as possible of its trajectories at the present stage of our liquid-modern, deregulated and disorganized, atomized and individualized, fragmented, disjointed and privatized society of consumers. All the same, given the attributes of the object, the result needs to be viewed as a career-report of an on-going voyage of discovery.

Our conversation, in a nutshell, has been about the specifically liquid-modern mode of evil – a mode arguably yet more menacing and treacherous than evil's other historical manifestations because of being fractured, pulverized, disjointed and disseminated; starkly distinct from its immediately preceding variety, concentrated and condensed as it struggled to be, as well as centrally administered. For that reason, the present-day liquidized evil is hidden from sight and avoids being spotted, as well as recognition for what it is and what it portends. Liquid evil has the awesome capacity for effective disguises and for recruiting human – all-too-human – concerns and desires to its service under false – yet exceedingly difficult to debunk and falsify – pretences. To add offence to the injury, quite a few recruits are seduced into volunteering.

In an enormous number of cases, liquidized evil manages to be perceived as a friend eager to help rather than a fiend; in Joseph Nye's terminology, it needs to be counted among the 'soft' – as distinct from 'hard' – powers, deploying temptation instead of coercion as its basic strategy, as in the case of contemporary multifaceted surveillance building a data bank millions of times more capacious than all the secret services of the solid-modern past could only dream of (and even then on condition of possessing extraordinary imagination) – from information supplied 24 hours a day and 7 days a week, voluntarily or unknowingly, by the users of cellular telephones, of credit cards, and by senders or receivers of computerized messages. No longer is the Ministry of Love needed to force people to take war for peace and coercion for care and friendly assistance.

Liquid evil, like all liquids, has the awesome capability of flowing around the obstacles rising or standing on its way. Like other liquids, it drenches them on its way, moistens, soaks and all too often erodes and dissolves – absorbing the solution in its own substance to further enhance its body. In addition to evasiveness, this capacity renders effective resistance to liquid evil yet more formidable a task. Having impregnated in the tissue of daily life and entrenched in its very core, evil, when (if) spotted, makes all alternative modes of life look implausible, indeed unreal; lethal poison presents itself duplicitously as a life-saving antidote to life's hardships.

Of these and other adjunct traits of liquid evil, in their many manifestations, we attempt to make a (by necessity incomplete, but hopefully preliminary) inventory. Our intention is to prime the canvas, rather than paint a complete picture. We hope to sketch the area yearning for research as comprehensive as it is urgent and equip it with some – in our belief useful – conceptual tools.

Z.B. & L.D.

Introduction: On Liquid Evil and TINA

Leonidas Donskis   We live in a world without alternatives. It's a world that proposes a single reality and a world that labels as lunatics – or, at best, eccentrics – all those who believe that everything has an alternative, including even the very best models of governance and the most profound ideas (not to mention business and engineering projects). The world has probably never been so inundated with fatalistic and deterministic beliefs as it is today; alongside serious analyses, as if from a horn of plenty, flow prophecies and projections of looming crises, dangers, downward spirals, and the end of the world. In this widespread atmosphere of fear and fatalism, the conviction arises that there are no alternatives to contemporary political logic and to the tyranny of the economy or to attitudes towards science and technology and the relationship between nature and humanity. Not by any stretch is optimism the foolish exultation that we are here in this place and that our surroundings are warm, fuzzy and comfortable; rather, it is the belief that evil is transitory and does not vanquish humaneness (or only briefly when it does). Furthermore, optimism means a belief that hope and alternatives do indeed always exist. The conviction that a pessimist is an all-round loftier and nobler being than an optimist is not simply a relic of the modern, Romantic sensibility and worldview – it is something greater.

This situation goes all the way back to the monumental conflict between Christianity and Manichaeism – after Augustine (who, by the way, defeated his inner Manichaean and became one of the Fathers of the Catholic Church). Christians held evil to be a state of errant or insufficient goodness that could be overcome, while Manichaeans held good and evil to be parallel but irreconcilable realities. Optimism is, above all, a Christian construction – it's based on the faith that good can overcome evil and that unexplored possibilities and alternatives can always be found. But we live in an age of pessimism. The twentieth century was excellent proof evil was alive and well, and this has reinforced the positions of modern Manichaeans. They saw a world that could be temporarily abandoned by God, but not by Satan.

One question, though, remains unanswered: how meaningful is Manichaeism today? Disbelief that God is all-powerful, and that He is Love, is something that might have been greatly reinforced in the wake of the many atrocities of the twentieth century. Mikhail Bulgakov's enduring work *The Master and Margarita* – written in 1928–41 and published, severely censored, in 1966–7 – is imbued with a Manichaean spirit: the novel makes numerous mentions of the concepts of 'Light' and 'Dark' developed by the Persian prophet and eponymous architect of this belief system. The interpretation of evil in this great twentieth-century East European novel (Kafka's *The Trial* is in my eyes the great Central European novel of the twentieth century) is one that asserts the self-sufficiency of evil. This interpretation of Christianity is close to that of Ernest Renan in his *Life of Jesus*, a study with which Bulgakov was quite familiar.

Even Czesław Miłosz considered himself something of a closet Manichaean. After his encounters with the incomprehensible evils of the twentieth century – which arose in a world no less rational and humanist than our own, which had created world-leading cultures (for example, in Russia and Germany) – Miłosz came to see evil as an independent and self-sufficient reality, or, at least, as a dimension that is not in any tangible sense affected by progress or modern forms of sensibility, nor by the world of in-depth theories. He noted that French philosopher Simone Weil was also a closet Manichaean: she conferred a millenarian meaning on the phrase 'Thy Kingdom Come' in the Lord's Prayer. There's a good reason why Miłosz taught a course on Manichaeism at the University of California, Berkeley. In his book *Miłosz's ABC*, he situated the opening act of twentieth-century evil in the story of

Bulgaria's Bogomils and the martyrdom of the Cathars in Verona and other Italian cities. All of the great East Europeans were Manichaeans to some degree – from Russia's Bulgakov through to George Orwell (who was an East European by choice).

Meanwhile, we live in an era of fear, negativity and bad news. There's no market for good news because no one is interested in it. (Although a fun and adventure-filled apocalyptic story is something quite different.) It is this that gives rise to the wholesale sowing of panic and the industry of fear – 'breaking news' that relies on commentaries with huge discrepancies, wherein the commentators often contradict themselves. Although some of these are occasionally insightful and well reasoned, most are hysterical and defeatist.

What does the concept of liquid evil signify? How can it be best understood these days when so many phenomena are made up of mutually exclusive qualities and characteristics? I would argue that liquid evil, contrary to what we could term 'solid evil' – the latter being based on a black-and-white social perspective, in which we can easily identify the resilience of evil in our social and political reality – assumes the appearance of goodness and love. More than that, it parades as a seemingly neutral and impartial acceleration of life – the unprecedented speed of life and social change implying the loss of memory and moral amnesia; in addition, liquid evil walks in disguise as the absence and impossibility of alternatives. A citizen becomes a consumer, and value-neutrality hides the fact of disengagement.

Individual helplessness and forsakenness, coupled with the state's denial and refusal of its responsibility for education and culture, go along with the heavenly marriage of neoliberalism and state bureaucracy, both of them insisting on the individual's responsibility not only for their life and choices in a free-choice-free world, but for the state of global affairs as well. In *Moral Blindness* (2013), you and I, Zygmunt, discussed a disturbing phenomenon, which I would describe as a post-academic university. An awkward amalgam of medieval academic ritual, specialization, a blatant and blunt denial of the role of the humanities in modern society, managerialism and shallowness sets a perfect scene for such a post-academic university, the playground for enormous pressures, the latter coming from technocratic forces disguised as the genuine voices of liberty and democracy – first and foremost, the market-oriented forms of determinism and fatalism, which leave no room for the idea of any alternative, including critical thought and self-questioning.

The mission and *raison d'être* of the post-academic university seem to lie in its overt shallowness, flexibility, submissiveness to the managerial elites, and also in adaptability to the calls and assignments coming from the markets and the political elites. Hollow words, empty rhetorics and countless strategy games appear as the quintessential form of this sort of tyranny of shallowness best embodied in the post-academic university. It is a strategy without a strategy, as the latter becomes merely a language game. The Wittgensteinian idea of language games was applied by Gianni Vattimo to describe technocracy walking in disguise as democracy, or today's politics without politics, all reduced to a series of language games. As you, Zygmunt, would have it in *Liquid Modernity* (2000), today's strategies without strategies, or politics without politics, are tantamount to ethics without morality.

'Outside the Church there is no salvation' (*extra ecclesiam nulla salus*) – this expression is ascribed to Saint Cyprian of Carthage, a bishop of the third century. We have a modern equivalent of this sort of civilizational logic, though, since ours is a corporate and quasi-medieval world where an individual does not have an existence outside of an institution which frames and moulds them. The Academia is the New Church nowadays. This is why the role of dissent, secular heterodoxy and the alternative in this world is far more problematic and complex than it may seem at first sight.

No alternatives are allowed. Privatization of utopia signifies the arrival of the new condition, under which no society is deemed to be good and just: only individual life stories can be success stories. As such, they tend to become our new utopian dreams in a utopia-free, or dystopia-ridden, world. TINA, or the acronym for There Is No Alternative (first forged by Margaret Thatcher, and then redefined and reinterpreted by you, Zygmunt), allows a point of departure when dealing with this uniquely new and unprecedented phenomenon – namely, one's ultimate belief in social determinism and market-based fatalism, the major difference between earlier decades and our time being the fact that, whereas Sigmund Freud's dictum informed us that biology is destiny, our dictum could be that the economy is destiny.

George Orwell saw clearly that the new forms of evil tend to walk in the guise of goodness and love. Thou shalt love Big Brother. Contrary to the predecessors of Oceania's Party – Jacobins, Bolsheviks and Nazis alike – no martyrdom is allowed. Your life will go unnoticed, and nobody will know anything about your existence. Or you will be swiftly and silently reformed to force you to assume and adopt the vocabulary that you had long denied passionately and consistently. Evil is not obvious and self-evident anymore. Low-intensity political oppression and human rights violation, as well as low-intensity military conflicts, obfuscate and obliterate the dividing line between war and peace. War is peace, and peace is war. Neither good news nor bad news remain un-ambivalent and clear nowadays: even if there is no war or any other calamity going on, it becomes impossible to discuss it without scaremongering, by the fear industry. Good news is no news. Bad news is *the* news by definition.

Therefore, when I refer to liquidity of evil, I mean that we live in a deterministic, pessimistic, fatalistic, fear-and-panic-ridden society, which still tends to cherish its time-honoured, albeit out-of-date and misleading, liberal-democratic credentials. The absence of dreams, alternatives and utopias is exactly what I would take as a significant aspect of the liquidity of evil. Two ideas of Ernst Bloch and Karl Mannheim proved prophetic: whereas Bloch regretted that modernity lost the warm and humane spirit of a utopian dream, Mannheim strongly felt that utopias were effectively translated into political ideologies, thus stripping them of alternative visions and confining them to the principle of reality, instead of imagination. The liquidity of evil signifies the divorce of the principle of imagination from the principle of reality, the final say being conferred upon the latter.

The seductive powers of evil are coupled here with disengagement. For centuries, as we know, the very symbol and embodiment of evil was the Devil, whether making his appearance as Mephistopheles in the legend of Faust – ranging from medieval tales to Christopher Marlowe's *The Tragical History of the Life and Death of Doctor Faustus* and Johann Wolfgang von Goethe's *Faust* – or as Woland in Mikhail Bulgakov's *The Master and Margarita*. This was the old news, though. The old 'good' Devil represented solid evil with its symbolic logic of the quest for human souls and active engagement in human and earthly matters. He simply pursued his goal trying to reverse and delegitimize the established social and moral order.

This is to say that solid evil was a sort of amorally committed and actively engaged evil, with a solemn promise of social justice and equality at the end of the time of the world. Liquid evil, on the contrary, comes up with the rationale of seduction and disengagement. Whereas Prometheus and Satan, according to Vytautas Kavolis, as we will see from the upcoming dialogue, were two protagonists of subversion, uprising and revolution, the heroes of liquid evil attempt to strip humanity of its dreams, alternative projects and powers of dissent.[1] In doing so, they act as protagonists of counterrevolution, obedience and submission. The logic of solid evil was to win the soul and to conquer the world by imposing the new rules of the game; yet the logic of liquid evil is to seduce and retreat, changing its appearances all the time. 'Seduce and disengage' – this is the very motto of the Proteus-like hero of both liquid modernity and of liquid evil. I know what is to be done, yet I refuse to engage, leaving my object or seduced victim to her or his own devices – that's the name of the game. From now onwards, drowning in the ocean will be called freedom.

Our freedom today becomes localized in the sphere of raw consumption and self-renewal. Control, surveillance, a dispositional asymmetry of power parading as freedom of choice, the fear industry and privacy exposure games make up the complex combination of the sociocultural condition that here we metaphorically call TINA and liquid evil. Promising all of humanity that you will allow and foster freedom, equality, justice, reason, pursuit of happiness, human rights, powers of individuality and association, social mobility, living without borders, and then disappearing suddenly, leaving individuals in their countless identity games mistaken for freedom, while also reminding them that it is up to them to solve the world's problems, without being able to rely much on institutions, fellowship and engagement – this is liquid evil's tried and tested strategy.

This is why I assume that the real symbol of liquid evil is a kind of Big Mr Anonymous, or collective Don Juan. Don Juan, in your eyes, Zygmunt, is modernity's real hero. Don Juan is the face of modernity, whose power lies in constant and incessant change. At the same time, his is the power of self-concealment and retreat for the sake of an asymmetry of power. Solid modernity was about the conquest of territories and their utilization for the sake of the state or any other power structure. Liquid modernity is about a hide-and-seek power game, be it a military strike followed by retreat or any other destabilizing action. Therefore, liquid evil, in terms of military campaigns, tends to disrupt the economy and life in certain territories or societies by bringing there as much chaos, fear, uncertainty, unsafety and insecurity as possible, instead of assuming responsibility and taking on the burden of remaking or transforming them. At this point, terrorism appears as a pure expression of liquid evil. Imperialism is about solid power games, yet terrorism is always about the liquidity of evil – even its sinister logic of speaking up in favour of society, coupled with disdain for a concrete society that is sacrificed for individualized power games, should not deceive us.

The seducer, who retreats by leaving a void, disenchantment or death, is a hero of liquid evil. The existential Don Juan comes to establish the asymmetry of power whose very essence lies in being able to observe the other without being seen. 'Chi son'io tu non saprai' ('Who I am you do not know') – these words from Wolfgang Amadeus Mozart's opera *Don Giovanni*, written by the librettist Lorenzo Da Ponte (who had Don Juan getting intimate with 2,000 women), reveal the crux of the modern manipulator's asymmetry. You do not see me because I will withdraw and leave you when it is no longer safe for me to stay with you and reveal too much of myself and my hidden suffering or weakness. Who I am you will never know, although I will find out everything about you. Yet there is an illusion left to the object of obscure desire that they will get as much attention and self-revelation as they could possibly need. An anonymous Internet comment delivering toxic lies, mortally wounding, hurting and brutally insulting us – that is, individuals with first and last names – is nearly a perfect expression of the liquidity of evil that operates on the ground and is deeply entrenched in our mundane practices. Who I am you do not know.

In this age of our painful quest for attention and of our obsessive, compulsive self-discovery and self-exposure, we constantly need a new promise and a repeatedly reinforced illusion that we – plain Janes or simple Simons – can gain world attention too.

Not just stars and world leaders but you, an ordinary mortal, can be important to someone because of the way you look or act or live or because of what you have or do or desire, or because of what you find funny or worth showing or talking about – in short, things all too human and easy to understand. We have begun acting like emigrants, even when we no longer set foot outside our own house or home town: thirsting for companionship and authentic human ties, we think that this, when it happens, is a short-lived miracle that will end soon – therefore, we must intensify this experience, for we don't know when it will come our way again.

Simply put, our freedom today becomes localized in the sphere of consumption and self-renewal but it has lost any connection with the most important thing: believing that you can change something in the world. This belief was shared by all the great prophets, theoreticians, ideologues and writers of modernity. Today all the great utopias have vanished. We are living in a period of dreary novels of warning and dystopias, though even the latter quickly turn into objects of easy, uncomplicated consumption. The sense of determinism and fatalism, strengthened not only by our failure to understand why and how economic systems crash and why we are beset by social crises, but also by our total dependence on far-away markets and currency fluctuations in distant lands, fosters the illusion that we as individuals are able to change things only by spontaneous reactions, acts of benevolence and compassion, kind words and intense communication. All that is left seems to boil down to technical instruments and more intense human relations. During outbreaks of the plague in Europe, the logic of carnivals, mass feasting and even orgies was predominant as well.

As you observed, Zygmunt, technology and social networks have become new forms of control and separation.[2] You see everyone; they all expose themselves, register and take part – fine: you only need to figure out how to keep everyone in a scheme in which there are no possibilities of hiding anything from the controlling structures of the state. Privacy is dying in front of our very eyes. It simply no longer exists – not only because there are no longer any messages unread and uncontrolled by outsiders or things that, as classical literature testifies, a human being had the right and even duty to take with himself to the grave. What has disappeared is simply what used to be rightly called a secret – it has become either a good traded over the counter, an object of exchange, a password to momentary and short-lived success, or else a weakness showing you have something to hide, thus enabling blackmail and the exertion of pressure to rob you of your last vestiges of dignity and independence. People no longer have secrets in the old, honourable sense, and don't even understand what that could possibly mean.

People gladly publicize their intimate life in exchange for momentarily having the spotlight turned on themselves: such feasts of exhibitionism are possible only in an age of unsteady, twittering connections and of unprecedented alienation. Some of those who expose themselves on Facebook are like those whose blogs resemble burps and belches in which they, full of narcissism, heave up their crises and frustrations; others are merely temporarily overcoming their feelings of isolation and insecurity. In this sense, Facebook was indeed a brilliant and timely invention, after all. Just when social separation and isolation became unendurable, when it was no longer bearable to watch bad television and to read the sadomasochistic press, Facebook came into the world.

But with it also came possibilities of mortal danger and fatal evil. For Facebook embodies, as you might say, the essence of the DIY phenomenon: do it yourself. Take off your clothes, show us your secrets – do it yourself, of your own free will, and be happy while doing it. DIY. Strip for me babe.

What has happened to our privacy? This question is being addressed nowadays with ever-increasing frequency. Of American society and its privacy crisis, Sarah E. Igo writes:

> Certainly, if recent popular titles are to be trusted – *The End of Privacy, The Unwanted Gaze, The Naked Crowd, No Place to Hide* (two different books!), *Privacy in Peril, The Road to Big Brother, One Nation under Surveillance*, and perhaps the creepiest entrant, *I Know Who You Are and I Saw What You Did* – we Americans are in the midst of an unparalleled privacy crisis. On one side are the Snowden revelations, Google Glass, drones, smart refrigerators, and commercial algorithms that seem to know us better than we know ourselves. On the other is the individual quest for self-exposure in an ever-expanding universe of social media: Here, it is not the state or corporations that seem to imperil privacy but, rather, willing exhibitionists, eager to dispense with the concept altogether as they share intimate details of their personal lives with strangers.[3]

There was a time when secret services and the political police worked hard to extract secrets and to get people to open up the details of their private and even intimately personal lives. Today these intelligence services should feel simultaneously exhilarated and unneeded: what should they do in a situation where everyone is telling everything about their own business themselves? But even if people don't disclose what they're doing, whom they dislike and how they got rich, they still willingly reveal who they communicate with and who they know. And it's impossible not to participate in that structure. If you leave it, you lose your sense of past and present, you sever contact with your classmates and your colleagues, you don't pay your dues, and you get separated from your community. In virtual reality and in Facebook, what vanishes is a fundamental aspect of real freedom: self-determination and a free choice of association rather than being sucked into a friendship simply because technology does not allow you to lead a civilized life otherwise.

But what does this say about our society? We are led to disturbing conclusions about human freedom no less than to an unwanted but warranted recognition that all of humanity is indeed becoming a nation that, though displaced and humiliated, is liked and hallowed: a Facebook nation. In the contemporary world, manipulation by political advertisement is capable not only of creating people's needs and their criteria of happiness, but also of fabricating the heroes of our time and controlling the imagination of the masses through successful biographies. These abilities make one pause for thought about a 'velvet' totalitarianism – a controlled form of manipulating consciousness and imagination that is cloaked as liberal democracy, which allows the enslavement and control even of the critics.

What remains deeply underneath is increasing social control and mass surveillance which reveals what happened to politics outpaced by technology. Whether we like it or not, technology does not ask us if we desire it. Once you can use it, you must do so. The refusal relegates you to the margins of society left without being able to pay your dues as a tenant or to participate in a public debate. The state which does not use mass surveillance becomes unable to justify its excessive use of secret services and spying techniques. Curiously, this tendency goes hand in hand with the spread and explosive proliferation of forms of self-display and confessional culture in general, whether in popular or even in highbrow culture.

With sound reason, then, Sarah E. Igo concludes:

> What if confessional culture is simply an avenue for turning the surveillance society inside out? One commentator writes that 'our physical bodies are being shadowed by an increasingly comprehensive "data body"', a body of data, moreover, that 'does not just follow but precedes the individual being measured and classified'.
>
> ... If this is the case, continuous visibility on one's own terms (whether through ACT UP, reality television, or Facebook) begins to look like a strategy – if not an unproblematic one – of autonomy, a public way of maintaining control over one's private identity. A culture of self-display may, in this way, be an obscure legacy of the 1970s, the outgrowth of identity politics and new media formats, but also a half-century's reckoning with data banks and bureaucratic surveillance.[4]

Therefore, technology will not allow you to remain on the sidelines. *I can* transmutes into *I must*. I can, therefore I must. No dilemmas permitted. We live in a reality of possibilities, not one of dilemmas. This is something akin to the ethics of WikiLeaks, where there is no morality left. It is obligatory to spy and to leak, though it's unclear for what reason and to what end. It works both ways – for and against the state – yet it never assumes responsibility for a truly anguished individual. It's something that has to be done just because it's technologically feasible. There's a moral vacuum here created by a technology that has overtaken politics. The problem for such a consciousness is not the form or legitimacy of power but its quantity. For evil (by the way, secretly adored) is where there is more financial and political power. If this is so, we deal a blow to ethics, since technology comes to fill the gaps left by politics and public morality: once you are connected, you are absolved and relieved. The media is the message, and living online becomes an answer to the dilemmas of our modern existence.

As mentioned, the net society is the fear-ridden society. It becomes a perfect place for the entire fear industry and organized scaremongering. It highlights and exposes the rise of technocracy disguised as democracy. At the same time, the net society and its public domain nourish and nurture such indispensable constituent parts of technocracy as value-neutrality and instrumentalism in all their manifestations. In this culture of constant fear, scaremongering, reform and incessant change, shallowness becomes an asset, rather than a liability. In fact, the culture of fear is the culture of shallowness, and vice versa. Yet shallowness is miscalled here adaptability and flexibility (just like 'simple truth miscall'd simplicity' in William Shakespeare's 66th sonnet). This results in shallow institutional practices, countless and meaningless strategy games, and empty rhetorics. Vocabularies become separated from concepts, and end up as senseless language games.

In 2013, you and I, Zygmunt, wrote together a book on the loss of sensitivity. The title of our book, *Moral Blindness*, was your idea, and it came out as an allusion to the metaphor of blindness masterfully developed in the novel *Ensaio sobre a cegueira* (Essay on Blindness) by Portuguese writer José Saramago. Yet the subtitle of our book, *The Loss of Sensitivity in Liquid Modernity*, came from my own theoretical vocabulary, albeit with your touch – your books would be unthinkable without the adjective 'liquid', be it liquid modernity or liquid fear or liquid love.

I recall the allusion you make in your works to the Nazi concept of 'life unworthy of life'. The phrase 'life unworthy of life' (in German, *lebensunwertes Leben*) was a Nazi designation for the segments of the populace which had no right to live. In our days, we witness a liquid-modern designation for the regions and countries whose tragedies have no right to break as news and whose civilian casualties or sufferings from political terrorism and violence have no right to change bilateral relations and trade agreements between Russia and major players in the EU.

Like Tibet with its series of self-immolations, Ukraine has become a litmus test case – as far as our moral and political sensibilities are concerned. How many more deaths and tragedies do we need to return us to our senses? What must the death toll be for us to switch on our sensitivities? We have a popular saying that the death of one person is a tragedy, yet the death of millions of people becomes a statistic. Unfortunately, this is more than true. The struggle between our moral blindness and our ability to see other individuals as ethical beings, rather than statistical units or a workforce, is the struggle between our own powers of association and dissociation, compassion and indifference, the latter being a sign of moral destructiveness and social pathology.

We learn from political history that we can withdraw from our ability to empathize with other individuals' pain and suffering. At the same time, we can return to this ability – yet it doesn't say a thing about our capability to be equally sensitive and compassionate about all troubled walks of life, situations, nations and individuals. We are able to reduce a human being into a thing or non-person, to be awakened only when we ourselves or our fellow countrymen are hit by the same kind of calamity or aggression. This withdrawal-and-return mechanism only shows how vulnerable, fragile, unpredictable and universally valid human dignity and life are.

These are the lessons to be learned or to be ignored again. This is why this book on the forms of evil, the old and the new, would be unthinkable, Zygmunt, without your conceptual adjective 'liquid'. It is a book about liquid evil, which surfaces and manifests itself far beyond any sort of theology and demonology of evil. The book is far more about evil situations and our mechanisms of disengagement and the abandonment of our sensibilities than about the supposed demons and fiends of our time.

Zygmunt Bauman   Indeed, a spectre is haunting Europe – the spectre of the absence of alternative.

Not for the first time had such a spectre appeared; its seminal novelty, however, is the globality of the world over which it hovers. In the centuries of territorial sovereignty and independence that followed the Westphalian settlement of 1648, the absence of alternative (in tune with the formula 'cuius regio eius religio' – the 'religio' to be subsequently replaced with 'natio') was confined to the space locked inside the boundaries of a single state; there were alternatives aplenty in the vast expanses starting on the other side of the borderline, and the territorial sovereignty was meant – first and foremost – barring such alternatives from crossing that line, by hook or by crook. The cracking and dismantling of the Berlin Wall, the twenty-fifth anniversary of which we've not long ago celebrated (that is, if one still remembers that celebratory hype – the liquid-modern memory span is shrinking fast), hammered home the blending of locally fixed spectres of TINA – 'There Is No Alternative' – into a global one.

As a matter of fact, such a process of blending was already fairly advanced well before the Wall had fallen. The earlier blending, however, undertaken and perpetuated inside the territorially sovereign supra-national camps, was still less than planetary because it was confined by the territorial limits mutually enforced onto each other by the reciprocally antagonistic camps – even if each of the two competing camps aspired to planetary domination. By laying wide open the heretofore off-limits and out-of-bounds sectors of the planet to the neoliberal member of the spectre siblings, the fall of the Berlin Wall inspired and propagated a Fukuyama-style mentality of the end of history. The centuries-old sibling rivalry between spectres, time and again lapsing into a fratricidal war, has finally reached its end – so it insinuated; and thus the victor, the neoliberal spectre, found itself left alone on the planet, no longer challenged and no longer forced to lean over backwards in order to keep in check, contain or convert its alternatives – now conspicuous solely by their impending absence. At least its prophets and apostles believed this to be the case. The two Bushes, father and son in quick succession, in cahoots with their respective British amanuenses Margaret Thatcher and Tony Blair, had to learn the faultiness and disingenuity of their conviction the hard – gory, shameful and humiliating – way.

In Europe, however, the brief – yet in its time unchallenged – rule of the TINA creed left lasting results, whose profundity and staying power remain still less than fully assessed. Steady dismantling of the network of institutions meant to defend the victims of the increasingly deregulated greed-driven economy, growing public insensitivity to rampant social inequality coupled with the incapacity of rising numbers of citizens – now abandoned (since no longer viewed as a potential danger to capitalist order and a seed of social revolution) to their privately possessed and controlled, albeit sorely and glaringly inadequate, resources and capabilities – resulted among the stake-holders of democracy (the actual – of the 'old Europe' – and prospective – of the 'new Europe') in a steady fall of trust in the ability of democratic institutions to deliver on their promises – in a stark opposition to the high hopes of the heady, optimistic aftermath of the Berlin Wall's crumbling. They also resulted in fast-stretching distance and a break in communication between political elites and the hoi polloi of whom the elites were meant – but neglected or failed – to be wardens. And so, paradoxically – or not that paradoxically, after all – the ostensible triumph of the democratic mode of human coexistence brought in practice an uncontainable wilting and fading of the public trust in its conceivable accomplishments. Such unprepossessing and depressing effects struck, even if in unequal measure, all member states of the European Union; they are, however, arguably, most poignantly felt in places in which the news of the Berlin Wall crumbling arose the greatest hopes: in the countries emancipating from the steely grips of the communist dictatorships to join the world of freedom and abundance.

No wonder that, as Ivan Krastev put it,[5] people are losing interest in elections and in whatever passes today for political controversy: 'There is a widespread suspicion that they have become a fool's game.' A game of pretences, I would say – with all the players aware of partaking in a prestidigitator-style racket of make-believe. Politicians pretend to be ruling, while the economic power holders pretend to be ruled. To keep in style, people drag themselves once every few years to the voting booths, pretending to be citizens. 'Managing the economy' is what is still left to the elected governments – but 'managing the economy' is one of those pretences to which politicians most eagerly resort: and no wonder – as the inevitable managerial failure may be all too easily explained away by recondite 'laws of the market' or similarly mysterious 'terms of trade'; and, as far as all facets of human life have already been reduced to their economic aspect, quantified in monetary terms and assigned a barcode, all and any failure to deliver on any promise may be explained away in such a manner. Galileo Galilei is reputed to profess that the book of nature is written in the language of mathematics. The book of society composed by the prophets and marketed by the apostles of neoliberalism, that 'hegemonic philosophy' (to use Antonio Gramsci's concept) of our times, has been written in the language of the economy; that book has been stored for safe-keeping in bank vaults – whereas the language in which it's written is to most of us, conveniently, no less – if not more – esoteric than the language of mathematics while being claimed to be legible solely to the bankers. But why does that kind of philosophy retain its hegemony? J. M. Coetzee, in a letter written on 29 March 2010 to his pen pal Paul Auster, gives us a hint: 'looking around us today, we see just what we might expect: we, "the world", would rather live through the misery of the reality we have created [...] than put together a new, negotiated reality'. To which words Auster replies, approvingly, a week later: 'This applies not only to economics but to politics and nearly every social problem we are faced with'.[6] This is precisely the case.

Is it therefore just a matter of our inborn inertia? Or perhaps, on the contrary, a contrived yet firmly settled novelty in our collective subconscious – whose praise we sing when awake, and with which we are taught, groomed and drilled to declare we have fallen in love (just as did the residents of Leonia, one of Italo Calvino's *Invisible Cities*, who insisted that 'their true passion is the enjoyment of new and different things', but – having been put off by 'yesterday's sweepings piled up on the sweepings of the day before yesterday and of all its days and years and decades', and horrified by the prospect of rubbish 'little by little invading the world'– were in fact truly passionate about 'the joy of expelling and discarding')? This is a moot question, to say the least, as both explanations have their valid claims to veracity. Whatever explanation of persistent hegemony we opt for, tracing it to its psychological foundations, it is the 'reality we have created', as Coetzee reminds us, that in the last account holds our thoughts and deeds in its steely grip. It draws stiff borders round our imagination, fixing by the same token limits to our will; it does it through dividing our options into plausible and fanciful. On the way, it downgrades and all but writes off our own preferences; when it comes to the visions of alternatives to the status quo and our resolve to pursue them, that 'reality we have created' wins hands down in competition with all other contraceptive drugs.

Politics, as we once knew it, used indeed the language of priorities – that is of preferred visions for the world. You bewail and mourn (as I do) the disappearance – the abandonment – of that language in public life. You see the demise of such language as one of the justifications – perhaps the paramount – for dubbing as 'post-political' the performances staged nowadays on the public arena. 'Selecting a priority' denotes, however, a gambit, a trigger or catapult, the first stage of an action; what about a reality as the one 'we have created', a reality that prevents the next stage from being reached, and, in the (unlikely) case an attempt to reach it were made, would assure its inefficacy and futility? We have created a reality in which the capability to act and the capability to decide which action needs to be given priority have been cast, and continue to be held, far apart. Our reality, I keep repeating, is marked by the divorce between power and politics. A sort of pincers, but in reverse: the power/politics pincers that used to cause incapacitation through being tightly locked, cause it now by having flown wide open: there is a yawning gap between the powers let free of political control and politics stripped of power – a void in which well-nigh everything can happen but nothing can be undertaken with confidence of success. I suspect that the growing and widening reticence to identify the priority tasks is unlikely to be overcome without finding an answer to the meta-puzzle of the twenty-first century, namely: assuming we know what needs to be done – who is resourceful enough and willing to do it?

One more comment: you and I are inclined to describe the present using the vocabulary of lacks and misses: 'this is no longer as it used to be', 'this or that disappeared', 'this or that is missing'. Our students (and hopefully quite a few of our readers) do not perceive in such terms the world which 'we' have created but 'they' found ready-made. As Michel Serres put it (with a bow to 'our' thinking habits),[7] 'they' no longer inhabit the same time: 'They are formatted by the media, which is broadcast by adults who have meticulously destroyed their faulty span of attention by reducing the duration of images to seven seconds, and the response time to questions to fifteen seconds'. 'We' may shudder when reading such (official!) figures, remembering, however vaguely, the times that favoured reflection, demanded patience and called for mental concentration and long-term purposes; I am tempted to say that such times are for 'them' a foreign country, but then I bite my tongue, recalling that not even 'foreign' means to 'them' – to the Internet-surfers since birth and of right – the same as it did (and still does) to 'us'. A question leaps, therefore, to mind: is it really so bizarre that the incipient majority of humanity, for-matted by the media and shrewd, pursuit-of-pleasure-promoting and pleasure-promising marketing techniques, views the public arena as an enormously expanded Woodstock-type stage or a timelessly extended TV sitcom; as a leisure-time entertainment, with a potential for keeping the viewers pleasurably amused – despite (or because of) being irrelevant to the humdrum prose of daily routine?

You vest your hopes of rebirth of fully-fledged democracy, of democratic institutions that genuinely represent the concerns and wishes of their electors, in a politics 'taking shape not in centres of power and in major capitals but first of all in the surrounding communities'. My off-the-cuff reaction: undoubtedly a good choice, but alas easier proposed than done. An investment better than most, alas waging the therapy of ailing democracy with resources themselves deeply in crisis and in need of resuscitation and convalescence. Before turning into an effective cure for the ailments of democracy in its present form, communities need to recover from their own disabling frailty.

Having in mind the doubtful adequacy of the idea of community bequeathed by our ancestors and invested in the morphology of present-day human associations, Serres suggests replacing the image of 'collectivity' with the notion of 'connectivity'.[8] Unlike collectivities, the 'connectivity' kind of human assembly is characterized by loose and eminently friable bonds, as well as by vaguely marked and immoderately porous boundaries. It is not by chance that the term 'community' tends these days to be replaced in common parlance by that of a 'network'. Unlike communities, networks are shaped and reshaped by the interplay of connecting and disconnecting, their contents and borders being for that reason perpetually *in statu nascendi* – underdetermined and unfixed. In jarring opposition to communities, they are easy to join and easy to leave; instead of negotiating the principles of their togetherness, as communities are forced to do by the fact of their compactness and ambitions of durability, networks tend to bypass the need to confer and enforce terms through the shortcut of splitting and separation followed by breaking off communication and reciprocal alienation. If the idea of 'community' is commonly associated with stability and continuity, 'network' associates with unsteadiness and impermanence. There is not much demand here for moral sensitivity, nor a promising start to democracy's recuperation and comeback.

The promotion of the spectre of the absent alternative to its present global status has brought in its wake one more – perhaps the most seminal – novelty: the falling apart of supra-nationally integrated blocks and the effacement of tight, fortified and impermeable borders able – or at least intended and pretending – to protect the principle of territorial sovereignty, put an end to the era of 'solid evil'. Evil amenable to concentration and monopolization by genuinely or putatively sovereign nation-states has spilled out of its nation-state containers – overflowing walls, however high and thick, and borders, however densely manned and power-fully armed. Most toxic and execrable categories of evil – stretch-ing from the bodily murderous, through socially devastating, to spiritually ruinous – can no longer be contained, let alone tightly sealed, in any container; they flow freely and easily penetrate each and any – natural or artificial – boundary. As I put it in *Liquid Modernity*, whereas solid bodies are, so to speak, space-defined and confined and therefore retain their shape, fluids

> 'flow', 'spill', 'run out', 'splash', 'pour over', 'leak', 'flood', 'spray', 'drip', 'seep', 'ooze'; unlike solid bodies, they are not easily stopped – they pass around some obstacles, dissolve some others and bore or soak their way through others still. From the meeting with solids they emerge unscathed, while the solids they have met, if they stayed solid, are changed – get moist or drenched.[9]

Over the recent years, evil has conformed, and continues to conform, to these fluid proclivities and habits.

1

From a Person to a Nonperson?

Mapping Guilt, Adiaphora, Precariousness and Austerity

Leonidas Donskis   The questions of guilt and repentance come to my mind immediately when I start thinking about this turbulent moment in our history. These questions were behind every piece of political change in the late 1980s that brought us the fall of the Berlin Wall and the collapse of the USSR. Yet these questions, as we all know, date back to post-war Europe.

Immediately after the Second World War, Karl Jaspers wrote a landmark study, *Die Schuldfrage* (The Question of Guilt, 1947), in which he addressed and articulated philosophically the question of German guilt.[1] As Jaspers felt that his nation had not only sinned gravely and mortally but also committed unspeakable crimes against humanity, the question of whether the nation *en masse* could be blamed and held accountable for war crimes was far from decidedly detached or naïve. It was against this background that Jaspers worked out a pattern for such a philosophical debate defining four categories of guilt: criminal, political, moral and metaphysical.

These four categories of guilt were specified and analysed by Jaspers: *criminal guilt* covers direct involvement in crimes and violations of laws; *political guilt* is inherited from political leaders or institutions whose actions we endorse as citizens – or, worse, political operators and the voices of lies and organized hatred; *moral guilt* arises from crimes against people, from which we cannot be absolved on the grounds of our political loyalty and civic obedience; and *metaphysical guilt* comes from staying alive, or doing too little or nothing to save the lives of our fellow human beings, when war crimes and other felonies are committed.

Jaspers insisted that, whereas the criminal and political guilt of Germans were directly related to crimes committed or orchestrated by flesh-and-blood individuals in Nazi Germany, moral and metaphysical guilt could be avoided by the generations to come, even if only because of the fact that Germans will continue sharing their language, a collective spirit and a sense of common history. As long as people retain their attachment and commitment to their society, they will have no way out of the predicament of today's guilt for the past, other than through internalizing the traumas their parents underwent.

The sense of guilt seems to have become a watershed between the post-war European ethos and a non- or anti-European mindset marked and permeated by blunt denial of any guilt due to one's nation's recent past. As the French philosopher Pascal Bruckner suggested in his provocative book *The Tyranny of Guilt*, an excess of guilt has become a characteristically European political commodity which is not necessarily linked to our genuine moral sensitivities – instead, it can be an ideological tool for silencing the opposing camp or stigmatizing the political elite we dislike.[2] This is especially seen in the case of Western Europe's colonial guilt, or in the case of American guilt for its racist past.

The strongest embodiment of the ethics of guilt in politics was German Chancellor Willy Brandt's moral *tour de force* when he knelt twice: first in the Warsaw Ghetto, Poland, and then at Yad Vashem (the World Centre for Holocaust Research, Documentation, Education and Commemoration, Israel) – a heroic and noble act of public repentance before the world for the crimes and sins of his nation. In fact, it was far from the gesture of a defeated foe, for there was no reason for Brandt to do this – the state is the state, and the individual, even if s/he happens to be its head, can hardly establish a public repentance or apology as a viable state policy.

Therefore, the state that kneels and apologizes, as in the case of Willy Brandt, violates the Hobbesian model of the modern state – the state that never admits its mistakes or regrets its faults, the state that never allows room for anything other than naked power. Power is truth, and truth is power – this is how the Hobbesian logic of power speaks. Evil is nothing but powerlessness. Whereas virtue lies solely in prowess and survival of the fittest, vice is all about weakness. International law and all norms and values are subject to change in accordance with a great power's top priorities and needs. We respect the sovereign whenever and wherever we see one, yet we despise any kind of No Man's Land (which we create, support and arm ourselves, to be able to disrupt any independent and dignified forms of life wherever they tend to appear), as human life there is nasty, brutish and short – this is the real message of the New Leviathan manufactured by Vladimir Putin's Russia.

Could we have possibly imagined the head of the former USSR issuing an apology for the heinous crimes and despicable conduct of its military, officials, the elite, and state machinery in general? Could we imagine any head of today's Russia ever offering an apology to the state whose existence they have undermined, if not ruined?

The answer is quite simple and clear – no. Germany and Russia are politically close only superficially. The pacifist society created in post-war Germany, coupled with their successful Ostpolitik in the twentieth century (which seems to have blinded the German political elite that lost its way in dealing with Putinism), poorly camouflages the fundamental difference between the two former aggressors, one of which has radically changed its paradigm in politics, while the other chose to stay the course in the ugliest way. For, whereas Germany chose to be the first truly non-Hobbesian state in the modern world, Russia has always been, and still continues to be, obsessed with how to revive and re-enact a predatory, unrepentant and profoundly immoral political world in the twenty-first century. Instead of Samuel Huntington's concept of the clash of civilizations, which underestimated the gulfs and moral abysses within Europe itself, we should try to understand the clash of two types of statehood, which is really what is at stake now. This is the clash of Thomas Hobbes and Willy Brandt in their new incarnations.

Another issue of utmost importance for our time is that of evil. This is something far more complex than the Devil in politics in terms of radical evil – we are able to tackle this sort of challenge. What lies underneath and is far more complex is what you, Zygmunt, would describe as liquid evil. I find this aspect of the problem crucial and central for the rest of our new dialogue, to be honest.

What does the Devil in politics signify? Does it make sense to switch to theology and demonology when discussing seemingly all-too-human aspects of modern life? History teaches us that it does make sense to do so. The twentieth century shows that the Devil in politics signifies the arrival of the forms of radical evil that openly devalue life, self-worth, dignity and humanity. They come to pave the way, instead, for fear, hatred and triumphing in someone else's destroyed freedom and self-fulfilment.

In his analysis of the emergence of the symbols of rebellion against / subversion of the established order, Vytautas Kavolis traced the symbolic designs of evil, understood as interpretive frameworks within which we seek answers to the questions raised by our time, in order to understand ourselves and the world around us.

Prometheus and Satan are taken here as core mythological figures and symbolic designs for revealing the concepts of evil that dominated the moral imaginations of pre-Christian and Christian thinkers and writers. Whereas Prometheus manifests himself as a trickster hero whose challenge to Zeus rests not only on his natural enmity to Olympic gods but on his compassion for humanity as well, Satan appears in the Bible as the one who subverts the universal order established by God, and, therefore, bears full responsibility for all manifestations of evil that result from this subversion.

Kavolis's work in cultural psychology provides a subtle and penetrating analysis of the models of evil as paradigms of secular morality, and of the models of rebellion as contrasting modes of cultural logic. In doing so, he offers his insights into the emergence of the myth of Prometheus and that of Satan. Prometheus emerges in Kavolis's theory of the rise of modernity as a metaphor for technological progress / technologically efficient civilization combined with a kind of sympathetic understanding of, and compassion for, the urges and sufferings of humankind. Satan is interpreted as a metaphor for the destruction of legitimate power, and for the subversion of the predominant social and moral orders.

In this way, Kavolis developed some of his most provocative and perceptive hints of how to analyse the symbolic logic of Marxism and all major social or political revolutions – aspects of which are at some points Promethean, and at others Satanic. Each modernity – for Kavolis spoke of numerous and multiple 'modernities', each of them as ancient as civilization itself – or civilization-shaping movement, if pushed to the limit, can betray its Promethean and/or Satanic beginnings.[3]

A valuable tool for literary theory and critique, this standpoint lay beneath Kavolis's insights into Herman Melville's *Moby-Dick* and Mary Shelley's *Frankenstein*. With sound reason, Kavolis noted that even the title of Shelley's novel, *Frankenstein, or the Modern Prometheus*, was deeply misleading – the obviously Satanic character, Frankenstein, who challenged the Creator of the universe and of the human being, was misrepresented there as a sort of modern Prometheus.

We employ, along with Prometheus and Satan, a gallery of literary personages and heroes who are the embodiments of our modern political and moral sensibilities: Don Juan, Don Quixote, Shylock, Othello or Macbeth. To these, I would add some historical persons, thinkers and writers, who came to shape our sensibilities, such as Niccolò Machiavelli, William Shakespeare or the Marquis de Sade. It is precisely within this interpretive context that Stendhal may well be credited for having deeply understood the philosophical meaning and cognitive value of the civilization-shaping characters, and their sensibilities, that are inseparable from the modern world.

Therefore, the Devil in politics is far from a fantasy. He comes into existence in many guises, one of them being the subversion and destruction of a universal – or at least a viable – social and moral order. Yet the Devil may appear as the loss of memory and sensitivity resulting in mass psychosis. Both aspects are richly represented and covered by modern Russia, the country whose writers strongly felt, and lucidly described, the touch of the radical evil whose essence lies in a deliberate rejection of human self-worth, dignity, memory and sensitivity, and our powers of association and compassion.

The Devil can strip a human being destined to become a nonperson and non-entity of their memory. By losing their memory, people become incapable of any critical questioning of themselves and the world around them. By losing the powers of individuality and association, they lose their basic moral and political sensibilities. Ultimately, they lose their sensitivity to other human beings.

The Devil, who safely lurks in the most destructive forms of modernity, deprives humanity of the sense of its place, home, memory and belonging.

Back when the movement for Lithuanian independence was just beginning, in the late 1980s, we encountered Georgian filmmaker Tengiz Abuladze's film *Repentance* and thought of it – this film about the invasion, by an almost Satanic totalitarian system, of the human soul, taking away its sensitivity and memory – as a sensation or even a miracle. The destruction of the ancient holy place in the city is synchronized with William Shakespeare's 66th sonnet, memorized by heart by the local murderer and dictator Varlam Aravidze and read by him to his future victims. It was a wonderful performance of an aria from Giuseppe Verdi's opera *Il trovatore* (the cabaletta *Di quella pira*).

After Aravidze's death, a woman appears whose family was murdered by the monster and who cannot come to terms with the idea that his remains should be peacefully returned to the land of Georgia. The film ends with the murderer's son, Abel, being convinced that something is not right and refusing to bury his father, having come to the realization that the loss of conscience and human sensitivity is too high a price to pay for remaining loyal. Because they fail to recognize the crimes of the past, the present fails to hold together for Aravidze's family and the entire nation, and the present becomes instead the hostage and victim of a lie. Abel Aravidze's son, the grandson of the murderer Varlam, is unable to bear the burden of shame and pain for the destroyed destinies of the townspeople, whose lives had become mere details or insignificant trifles in the family's stories about their proud past and heroism.

I am talking about the Shakespearian dilemma that the Georgian film director understood so well in presenting his immortal film. What is more important: the historical tale which inspires the town and raises morale among its citizens, or the truth and conscience? Can these things in general coexist peacefully? Should small details and unimportant matters – which you will in any case not be able to preserve for the whole of the people with whom the current and future generations must live – be sacrificed for the sake of the heroic narrative?

In your books, Zygmunt, you have developed the theory of the adiaphorization of consciousness. During times of upheaval or intense social change and at critical historical junctures, people lose some of their sensitivity and refuse to apply the ethical perspective to other people. They simply eliminate the ethical relationship with others. These others don't necessarily become enemies or demons, they are more like statistics, circumstances, obstacles, factors, unpleasant details and obstructing hindrances. But at the same time they are no longer people with whom we would like to meet in a 'face-to-face' situation, whose gaze we might follow, at whom we might smile, or to whom we might even return a greeting in the name of recognition of the existence of the Other.

People who have lost their sensitivity, temporarily or for a long time, are no demons. They simply remove from their sensitivity-zone certain people or entire groups. As the Greek Stoics of antiquity and later religious reformers and thinkers in the Renaissance believed, there are things which are in reality inessential and unimportant, matters over which there is no point in arguing or crossing swords. This kind of unimportant thing is called an *adiaphoron* – Greek neuter singular, ἀδιάφορον, from ἀ- (a negative prefix marker) + διάφορος ('different'), making 'indifferent' – and the plural is *adiaphora*. An example of its use is found in the letter that Philipp Melanchthon wrote to Martin Luther in which he said the Catholic liturgy was an adiaphoron, hence it was pointless to argue about it with the Catholics.

On 27 April 1942, George Orwell writes in his *Wartime Diaries* about how selective human attention, memory and sensitivity can be. According to him,

> We are drowning in filth. When I talk to anyone or read the writings of anyone who has any axe to grind, I feel that intellectual honesty and balanced judgment have simply disappeared from the face of the earth. Everyone's thought is forensic, everyone is simply putting a 'case' with deliberate suppression of his opponent's point of view, and what is more, with complete insensitiveness to any suffering except those of himself and his friends.... Everyone is dishonest, and everyone is utterly heartless towards people who are outside the immediate range of his own interests. What is most striking of all is the way sympathy can be turned on and off like a tap according to political expediency.[4]

Orwell aptly describes here the mechanism of value- and ethics-neutrality which originates in our ability to be selective when dealing with human anguish and suffering, and which lies in our propensity to turn on and off our sensitivity, as if it was a mechanism controlled by a skilled operator, instead of a sensible and sensitive human being. A silent agreement to abandon and reject the ethical dimension in human exchanges is the very essence of adiaphora.

We discussed this phenomenon in our book *Moral Blindness*.[5] This withdrawal-and-return mechanism (to borrow and slightly remake Arnold J. Toynbee's term from his *A Study of History* (1935)) only shows how vulnerable, fragile, unpredictable and universally valid human dignity and life is. Yet there is another disturbing phenomenon deeply entrenched in the forms of liquid evil – namely, the immoral political opportunists walking in the guise of martyrs and dissenters for whom fascism, radical nationalism or any other similar form of contempt for freedom and human dignity appears as a mere possibility to *épater la bourgeoisie* ('shock the bourgeoisie'). What lurks beneath such a stand is a total moral void and shamelessness.

The Russian writer Eduard Limonov, notorious for his apparent firing of a machine gun at a besieged Sarajevo, as well as for his adventurous and flamboyant life in New York and Paris, contrived not only to set up a neo-fascist political party in Russia, which was for some time in fierce opposition to the Kremlin and Vladimir Putin, but also to attract Russian liberals and democrats – before finally accepting Putin as his true hero. What a long and winding road it was from fascism to fascism, via bohemia and dissent.

In his fictionalized memoir, *It's Me, Eddie*, Limonov wrote: 'I have no shame or conscience, therefore my conscience doesn't bother me.'[6] With sound reason, then, Masha Gessen writes of Limonov:

> His lack of convictions is typical of people who grew up in the Soviet Union, where survival depended on being finely attuned to the ever-changing Party line. The difference is that most people in the USSR, and in Putin's Russia, change their views in order to fit in while Limonov generally changed them so as to differ from the majority position at the moment.[7]

We could well echo Immanuel Kant's idea of 'unsocial sociability'[8] by offering another oxymoron, such as, for instance, 'morally

uncommitted commitment' or 'politically disengaged engagement', to describe the phenomenon of Eduard Limonov as being
characteristic of profound immoralism devoid of the sense of guilt
and shame – in a way, not dissimilar to the effects of adiaphorization of consciousness. Limonov chose to side with evil only to
differ from the majority. Paradoxically – albeit logically enough
– he did so only to find himself amidst the crowd that was over-
whelmed by mass psychosis.

Zygmunt Bauman   To a journalist's question 'How does it feel
to be called to St Peter's office?', Jorge Mario Bergoglio answered
in one word: sinful. I guess he meant more than repeating the
Church dogma of carrying his own share of Adam and Eve's
original and hereditary sin (a dogma invented and canonized by
the Church with the casting of its members in the status of 'debtors
a priori', and itself in that of 'a-priori creditors', in mind); my
guess is that, when giving such an answer, he was closer to
the raising of Jaspers's concept of metaphysical guilt to its fully
and truly universal status – an act all but unavoidable in the
present-day globalized (and as Ulrich Beck would say 'cosmopoli-
tized') world of time–space compression: the world of *universal
interdependence*.

As José Saramago noted on 9 October 2008,[9] quoting his own
Lanzarote *Notebooks* of 1990: 'God is the silence of the universe
and man is the cry that gives meaning to that silence.' The meaning
given by the man whose present name is Pope Francis to the continuing silence of the universe, I surmise, is the *universality* of
guilt. We – humans – having taken the world a few centuries ago
under human management, consequently bear responsibility for
all and any evil malpractices, wherever and whenever they are
perpetrated by the Devil or his earthly emissaries or hirelings; we
bear that responsibility whether we accept it or not, and whether
we seek atonement and roll up our sleeves to clean our estate of
evil, or refuse to do the penance and plunge deeper into iniquity.
In the language of Gospels, we are all sinful. In lay language,
we are all guilty. It is when switching to that second language
that we pulled Prometheus from his original opposition to the
Messiah and stood him, unambiguously, in the role of the tamer/
conqueror of evil. This considered, choosing the denomination
of 'the Modern Prometheus' for Frankenstein was *not* 'deeply

misleading'. Retrospectively, that decision taken by Mary Shelley in 1818 feels, on the contrary, uncommonly insightful – indeed prescient of what would have become nearly common sense in the times following the fratricidal horrors of the thirty-year-long war of European nations started on the planetary stage 100 years earlier by the European masters of the planet and standard-bearers of civilization. We've tried quite recently to recall – and to re-think and re-feel through – the shock which that war must have been for people still gullibly unaware of the full range of Prometheus' capabilities. This brings me to the issue of memory; an issue you raise, saying that 'losing their memory, people become incapable of any critical questioning of themselves and the world around them'.

My first reaction is: how true! But a moment later comes a reflection: yes, a truth has been told, but not the whole truth – because the critical capacity escapes humans in no lesser a measure when they lose the ability to *forget*. Memory is a double-edged sword: a blend of the blessing with a curse. It enslaves as much as, and perhaps more often than, it liberates; it may be deployed in the service of life as readily as harnessed to the chariot of death. All the more so for being, endemically, incapable of reaching and retaining completeness: unable to preserve and retell history as Leopold von Ranke wished it to be retold – *wie ist es eigentlich gewesen*; for being, on the contrary, incurably selective, partial and militantly, pugnaciously partisan – and thus instrumental in both eye-opening and eye-shutting operations.

These two faces of memory have been all too well documented over the years to require a novel elaborate argument. I'll limit myself therefore to but one, a most recent example, borrowed from Ivan Krastev's essay '1914 Versus 1938: How Anniversaries Make History', published in the *Open Democracy* journal on 7 July 2014. Having asked why the West is so reluctant to announce Putin's invasion of Ukraine as a case of war, Krastev finds the answer in bookshelves overflowing with learned studies, opinion-making press with occasional opinion articles, and TV screens with historical documentaries – all leaning over backwards to capitalize on the hundredth anniversary of the 1914 catastrophe, and proclaiming, in unison, the Great 1914–1918 War as acciden-tal, caused by 'misunderstanding, miscommunication and the lack of trust between the Great Powers' of the day; all resulting in a 'collective suicide of Europe' through an 'overreaction' glaringly incommensurable with a single pistol shot let off in Sarajevo by a neurotic youngster, which triggered the universal mobilization of millions-strong armies. Were Putin's annexation of Crimea to coincide with an anniversary of 1938 – so Krastev suggests – reactions in Europe would have been quite different; that year has, after all, been recorded in our collective memory as the year of an exercise in 'appeasement' of a single-minded, unfaltering and unscrupulous aggressor – as foolhardy as it was pointless, and in the end disastrous and all but suicidal. By the way, Krastev suggests as well that if the fall of the Berlin Wall had not coincided with the anniversary of the 'Marseillaise' and 'Liberté, Égalité, Fraternité', the event could have run a somewhat different course and been recorded by the historians and inscribed in public memory under a somewhat different name. In both cases – as in another case under his microscope, that of Kennedy's dilemma in the handling of the 'Cuban Crisis' – Krastev, in my view, has a point – a quite strong point, as a matter of fact. The question is: are all such considerations good or bad tidings for the value of the impact that the work of memory – selective remembrance and selective forgetfulness – has on our collective reflexive and critical abilities? I am afraid we will need to wait for a reliable and trustworthy answer till another (which one?) anniversary – another reason to approach with due circumspection the verdict on the balance between benedictions and damnations in the notoriously Janus-faced and double-tongued public memory.

You ask: 'Does it make sense to switch to theology and demonology discussing seemingly all-too-human aspects of modern life? History teaches us that it does make sense to do so.' I fully agree. You and I are not the first to note that the mind-set in which the hegemonic philosophy of modern politics is framed is but a slightly altered mind-set of theology; Niccolò Machiavelli was arguably the first to declare the interests of a political body to be prior to morality and religious commandments – but this heresy has been turned into the orthodoxy by modern political theory and practice. One of the very few accomplishments of Carl Schmitt with which I am in full agreement was the presentation of (modern) politics as eminently amenable to a theological treatment. Schmitt showed the modern idea of the 'sovereign' to be a secularized version of the timeless idea of God: by definition, a ruler who, while being guided in his actions solely by the *Staatsräson*, is fully, and uniquely, entitled (and consequently also the only one able) to decide what that 'reason of the State' consists of, what it commands us to do, how it instructs us to proceed, and who its enemies are – who must be for that reason swept out of the way. The sovereignty of the sovereign, like that of God, is the decisionist prerogative incarnate: neither of the two absolute rulers owes his subjects (or anybody else for that matter) explanation of his motives and reasoning – let alone an apology for his deeds. In the Book of Job, God speaking 'out of the tempest' (he is the only one who does so) sets the procedure: 'I will ask questions, and you shall answer' (Job 40, 7) – not the other way round. And at the end of God's lengthy monologue, Job answers: 'I know that thou canst do all things and that no purpose is beyond thee. But I have spoken of great things which I have not understood, things too wonderful for me to know. [...] Therefore I melt away; I repent in dust and ashes' (42, 2–3, 6). The sole thing left to man's decision is to make sure that a command came from The Almighty – be it God or the Sovereign ruler. This is the point at which human responsibility originates and, for all practical intents and purposes, ends: responsibility *to* the superior *for* obedience to the command and for desisting to disobey. There is, however, no responsibility for the *content* of the command – whose rationale, wisdom, benefits or other relative merits may well stay beyond human comprehension; understanding of the merits and demerits of that content lies neither in the power nor in the duty of the executor of God's or the Sovereign's will. This scheme of reasoning may not answer the question *unde malum?*, but it goes a long way towards explaining why decent, chaste, pious – indeed, moral – people do happen to engage in such massive numbers – earnestly, even if not whole-heartedly – in perpetrating evil deeds. And this is, by the way, why Levinas insisted that, rather than deriving the morality of acts from the 'needs of society' (whatever that basket-like notion may be contrived to mean), we should set society on the defendant's bench in the tribunal of ethics. And this is why Hannah Arendt averred that the sole way to stay moral is to be disobedient (to put it bluntly: to place commands of morality above all others, whatever the cost).

Seminal departures have happened, however, since Levinas or Arendt wrote what they did: something tremendously important

– the passage from 'solid' to 'liquid' modernity, from a society of producers to a society of consumers, from the 'totalizing' body politic to its 'individualizing' alternative, and all in all from a 'regulating' to the 'deregulating' society. Ours are the times of the *crisis of sovereignty* – whether in its original divine, or its updated secularized/laicized, incarnation.

One of the consequences of those shifts has been to render redundant mass participation in state-initiated, state-commanded and state-monitored evils. We no longer have massive conscription armies; murder has turned into a task for professional soldiers – and those professionals have turned mostly into fully programmed attachments to smart technological contraptions. This seems to come close to the once-popular ironic vision of future factories, expected to employ only two live creatures: one man and one dog – the man will be there to feed the dog, and the dog to prevent the man from touching anything. Smart missiles and drones have chased away battleships and fighter pilots. Ever more seldom do the killers face the killed – and so the demands of obedience come into direct confrontation with moral scruples much less often than they used to – if at all. As a result, all the arguments once advanced to trace the social roots of evil now lose some of their past explanatory power. In order to locate and explore the present-day shelters or fortresses, laboratories or farmsteads, of evil, we need – I suggest – to bring into our attention some heretofore left-out-of-our-sight features of the modern mode of being-in-the-world.

From its start, modernity declared and waged a war on the strenuous and onerous aspects of human existence. The 'promise of modernity' was the vision of life free from discomfort and inconvenience; a life making difficult tasks easier to perform; of effective actions demanding less arduous training; of ratios of results to time-and-energy expenditures constantly rising, and the distances separating desires from their satisfaction evermore shrinking; all in all, the promise of making life easier, less and less cumbersome, discomfiting and annoying. That, obviously, meant a promise to eliminate, one by one, all or at least most of the objects and situations that caused or were deemed to cause – whether by design or by default – discomfiture and annoyance. Originally, in the times when amelioration of human conditions was viewed as a job to be performed by states and municipalities, engaged respectively in the construction of 'good societies' and hospitable, orderly, secure and user-friendly social settings, the task of fulfilling the promise was laid at the door of powers-that-be – states and their delegated plenipotentiaries. Subsequent history, however, following the overall individualizing trend, shifted the task from the realm of governmental concerns and politics to the new area of 'life politics' (so dubbed retrospectively by Anthony Giddens), relegated and left to the undivided private responsibility of the individual members of society and the resources at their command (in Ulrich Beck's pithy rendition, each individual *de jure* – that is, each of us – is now expected to find and deploy individual solutions to socially created troubles; let me add that this new expectation has replaced the now bygone antici-pation of social solutions to individually suffered troubles). Inten-tionally or inadvertently, we – the individuals-by-the-decree-of-fate – have been burdened with order-building tasks previously per-formed by the state, endowed with the right to apply on our own initiative and according to our own – private – criteria, the sort of 'order' we choose to pursue. It is individual comfort – wellness and satisfaction – that has been elevated to the rank of legitimate (as well as right-and-proper) cause of and reason for action.

I believe this seminal shift has become one of the principal sources of the 'liquidized' form of social evil – fractured, pulver-ized, disjointed and disseminated, starkly distinct from its previous one, concentrated and condensed as well as centrally adminis-tered. The former variety of evil, foregathered, amassed and firmly held as it was in the hands of the state, which claimed the monop-oly on the means of coercion (a monopoly by now – in the times of 'outsourcing' and 'contracting out' of state functions to the free-for-all competition of market forces, unbridled and exempted from state control – all but abandoned and forgotten), promoted – as a sort of a side effect – human solidarity (albeit confined in the state boundaries); the collateral damage done by the evil dis-seminated, and trickling down or 'subsidiarized' to the realm of individually managed 'life politics' and/or transferred to the free-for-all of the deregulated markets released from political supervi-sion, promotes competition and rivalry, enmity and mutual distrust, estrangement and distance-keeping, as well as the attitude of 'Catch as catch can', and 'The winner takes it all' – all in all, 'Everyone for himself, and Devil takes the hindmost.' Evil lies in wait and in ambush in the countless black holes of the thoroughly deregulated social space – in which cut-throat competition and mutual estrangement have replaced cooperation and solidarity, while forceful individualization erodes the adhesive power of inter-human bonds. Evil has found its shelter *in the seams of the canvas woven daily by the liquid-modern mode of human interaction and commerce*, in the very tissue of human cohabitation and the course of its routine daily reproduction. In its present safe houses evil is hard to spot, to unmask, to extract and evacuate. It jumps out without warning and hits at random, with no rhyme and reason. The result is a social setting comparable to a minefield, which we know to be full of explosives and in which we are quite sure explosions sooner or later must happen, and yet we are unable to guess when and where.

Jean-Claude Michéa asked a fully and truly fundamental question:

> How is it possible to escape the war of all against all, if virtue is simply a mask for self-love, if no one can be trusted and if one can only count on oneself? This is decidedly the inaugural question of modernity – this strange civilization that, for the first time in History, has set out to base its advances on methodical distrust, fear of death, and the conviction that loving and giving are impossible acts.[10]

The answer to the above question offered by neoliberalism, the hegemonic philosophy of liquid-modern deregulation, is to seek a way out from that horrifying predicament in putting a wager on human self-interest; if only coupled with Kant's categorical imperative – so that philosophy suggests – the decision to let self-interest do its job without interference would promote 'empiricism and moderation'; it would mitigate and cool down ghastly, macabre passions and emotions, that prime cause and natural habitat of evil. It won't put paid to the evil endemic to the human condition; but, 'equally distant from religious fanaticism and utopian reverie, neither City of God nor City of the Sun', it will lead to 'the least bad society possible', 'protect humanity from its ideological demons, by offering the incorrigible egoists that all men are the means to finally live in peace and pursue their prosaic occupations in tranquility'.[11]

Well, that 'least bad society possible' has proved, in practice, to be over-flown by evils all of its own variety and creation. The brave new City of Men, or rather City of Loners – of solitary, self-referential beings let loose by fading and wilting, eminently revocable and disposable, inter-human bonds, ensconced in cocoons of self-care and self-interest (each one in its own, just like the sailor in Edgar Allan Poe's *Maelstrom* who sought salvation from the raging licentious elements in a barrel too small to provide shelter for more than just the one castaway), of individuals preoc-cupied body and soul with the staunchly centripetal pursuit of personal 'wellness', the contorted relic of whatever remained of moral commands and impulses after the privatization of concerns, commitments and obligations – that City of Loners only 'liquid-ized' the once solid, petrified evil of the City of God or City of Sun, detracting nothing from its former gall and venom. If solid evil – the evil expropriated, sequestrated, condensed and monopo-lized by cardinals, princes, tyrants and fraudulent saviours – squashed human society and reduced it to a pulp, its liquid variety soaks and saturates it after the pattern of capillary blood vessels, seeping into, settling in and oozing to and from its individual cells.

The 'liquidization' of evil – its deregulation, dissemination, privatization – impressed its stamp on all and any variants of evil and any category of evil-doing, while at the same time rendering resistance to evil more difficult and active participation in its reproduction more likely. What follows is but a random sample of cases of such impacts – drawn from among the most recent consequences of evil's 'liquidization'. Having written, for the last thirty years (most recently in *Liquid Life* (2005) and *Collateral Damage* (2011)), quite a lot about evil's many incarnations in the course of human history, and about the causes of its stubborn presence and vigour, and not wishing to repeat myself, I'll confine myself here to the new developments which in my past publica-tions were not (and could not have been) recorded.

Take the bane widely bewailed under the label of 'brainwash-ing'. That term has had a spectacular career since it first appeared in print in an article published by Edward Hunter, a journalist on the *Miami News*, on 7 October 1950. The rather convoluted history of the concept to which this term refers reaches, however, deep into the Chinese tradition of Taoist teaching – going as far back as the 2700s BCE and ascribed to the legacy of the writings of Laozi and Zhuangzi. Taoism instructed its followers to cleanse their hearts and minds of the dregs and muck of mundane quotidian life to make themselves fit, ready and deserving to enter the sublime universe of the holy; that idea was recycled millennia later by Mao, into the postulate of expurgating hearts and minds of the leftovers of the reactionary mind-set in order to deserve membership of the emergent classless communist society (another term commonly used in Maoist China for that operation was 'turning over').

As a matter of fact, the Taoist idea may be viewed as a case of a much wider – indeed, a well-nigh universal – cultural phenomenon, described by Victor Turner[12] as the 'rite of (symbolic) passage' from one social allocation/condition to another (for instance, from youth to adulthood, or from bachelorship to marital status). Between the starting point and the destination, there needs to be a 'transitory stage' of a 'limbo', a 'no-man's land' – a symbolic 'social nakedness' of sorts: all trappings and paraphernalia of the status about to be abandoned need to be expropriated – stripped, removed, wiped out and swept away – before the badges of the status to be assumed are put on:. Those making the passage need first to be bared naked – indeed, radically cleansed of the traces of the past – in order to be admitted to their new social identity. This is something like clearing a site for the construction of a new building – though in this case the object of construction is the human mind-set.

The phenomenon of 'brainwashing' is eminently present nowadays in both propaganda and commercial advertising – though hiding under the politically correct names of 'advertising', 'broadcasting', 'public relations', downright to 'information service', and resorting to Joseph Nye's 'soft', instead of 'hard', variety of power. Now, as then, brains must be 'washed' before they can be re-filled. Spin doctors hired by incumbent and aspiring politicians, and Vance Packard's 'persuaders' in the service of marketers have learned their lesson well and lifted their art to new heights beyond the imagination of Hunter and his Chinese inspirers.

The quality of being hidden, covert, evasive, subterranean, unspottable, unpinpointable – for all practical intents and purposes, invisible, and for that reason redoubtable, irresistible and in all probability invincible – amounts, however, to a new, fully and truly watershed leap in the history of brainwashing technology. We are tightly wrapped in a spidernet of electronic surveillance, and, knowingly or not, willingly or not – in any case, without being asked permission – drawn into the role of the spiders who weave it, or their docile and all-too-often zealous acolytes. Contemporary brainwashing presents that curse as a blessing in disguise: the manifest function of the algorithms, the principal weapon of present-day brainwashing, is – to quote Luke Dormehl – 'allowing us to navigate through the 2.5 quintillion bytes of data that are generated each day (a million times more information than the human brain is capable of holding) and draw actionable conclusions from it'.[13] The apparent blessing suggested by such functions is the hope that the computers with their in-built algorithms will carry us safely over the oceans of data in which we would drown if we tried to swim (let alone to dive) on our own (indeed, one enquiry to Google will dazzle you with the rebarbative, daunting, impassable vastness of those waters). The latent curse, however, is that those of 'us' allowed to navigate through the oceans of data tend to be, in the first place, the powers-that-be – the powers that monitor us – and the 'actionable conclusions' drawn by these kinds of navigators allow them to pinpoint each one of us individually in order to flawlessly target us for the benefit of their – unmonitored by us – purposes: purposes such as forcing or alluring us to part with our money, enlisting us for causes not of our choice, or targeting us for the next round of drones.

Indeed, the inclination to present a curse as a 'blessing in disguise' is the constitutive, defining feature of the present-day technology of brainwashing. Surveillance in the name of the security of the surveilled is perhaps its most emblematic and conspicuous example. Let me recount a recent experience of my own. A few days ago I happened to need to change planes inside the same (5th) terminal at Heathrow Airport. In the few hundred yards separating the gate at which I landed from the gate from which I was scheduled to fly away, I was subjected to five (five!) separate security checks – each one boasting cutting-edge technology while similarly humiliating: involving oodles of unflattering snapshots, bodily searches, partial undressing, taking off trouser belts and shoes, spreading or lifting legs, etc. At the end of my calvary, shared with thousands of my co-sufferers thoroughly stripped of the shreds of dignity, I was confronted with a huge billboard

proudly documenting, in colourful statistical graphics, the acco-
lade bestowed on the airport by its users, grateful for its care of
their safety and well-being. Aside that billboard, there were somewhat less user-friendly announcements: for instance, 'You should
be able to lift your luggage up to the overhead closets unassisted';
or 'allowing enough time for reaching the gate before the end of
boarding' is your responsibility (whereas the numbers of departure
gates were indicated on monitors 20, or even fewer, minutes before
departure). Passengers seasoned to swallow without murmur the
first travesty were obviously hoped to be ready to view such new
hardships as manifestations of the user-friendliness of the service.

The above case of brainwashing is common and forthright
enough to have been widely noted, described and familiarized; it
is, indeed, trivial to the point of having been by now accepted as
unavoidable and irresistible. In our collective consent to it, we at
the receiving end of brainwashing have signed a blank cheque for
further unstoppably rising and refining surveillance technology
camouflaged in the 'care for security' garb – a technology used
principally for purposes fairly remote from, if at all related to,
safety concerns. There are, however, innumerable cases of a kind
of '*indirect* brainwashing', or a 'brainwashing *by proxy*' technique
– or, perhaps, of a latest rendition of Orwell's 'doublespeak' (that
is, deliberate distortion or downright reversal of words' meanings), an old procedure now, with its social impact and efficiency
inflated and boosted by the unprecedented swing, density and
momentum of its deployment. An example, for instance, is what
I recently saw displayed on a giant screen inside Amsterdam's
Schiphol Airport.

What I saw there was on one of the numerous giant screens
transmitting the 24-hours-a-day 7-days-a-week broadcast of the
CNN 'news'. Whatever the 'news' at the moment, it was inter-
rupted every 10 minutes or so by the self-promotion of the
Company, assuring the viewers that 'CNN connects the world'.
Between the interruptions, pictures were shown of a catastrophe
in one place, a murder in another, a court trial in yet another, a
communal dance in appropriately exotic surroundings, as well as
heads of all skin colours talking in yet more bizarre sceneries.
CNN was connecting nothing, let alone 'the world'; it was instead
slicing and splitting the image of the planet into myriads of disjointed and scattered bits and pieces too briefly shown to be taken

in, let alone digested, and chopping lived time into a multitude of disconnected and dispersed snippets. In that flow of images and words there was neither continuity nor consistency; most certainly, there was no logic. By design or by default, one of the foremost and most widely watched broadcasting companies has trained its viewers to watch without understanding, and listen without comprehension; to consume information while neither seeking nor expecting to find its meaning, causes or consequences. The overall lesson divulged from the screen was pretty straightforward: the world is a chaotic aggregate, or rather incessant flow, of dismembered and dislocated fragments with little, if any, rhyme or reason – and nothing can be done to make sense of it, let alone to make it more amenable to reason and reason-guided preventing, amending or rectifying actions.

Orthodox brainwashing was aimed at clearing the site of the relics of old logic and sense, so as to make it ready for the construction of new logic and sense. Present-day brainwashing is keeping the site permanently void and barren, admitting nothing more orderly than a haphazard scattering of tents as easy to erect as to dismantle. It is no longer a one-off purposeful undertaking, but a continuous action holding its own continuity as its sole purpose.

Now let me present another case. The great playwright and story-teller Anton Chekhov, known for his mastery of fishing crystal-clear logic out of the muddied waters of life's illogicality, appraised his fellow truth-seekers that if a gun is hanging on the wall in the first scene of a play, it must be fired by the third at the latest. By bringing that logic into view, Chekhov put his finger, inadvertently, on one of the two major reasons for the spectacular incidents of violence occupying ever-expanding space among the realities, and in the prevailing imagery, of the present-day world. Courtesy of the cutting-edge, while profits-greedy, arms industry – whole-heartedly supported by high-GNP-figures-greedy politicians, even though it evades their half-hearted attempts at controlling its order-books – guns hung on walls are nowadays aplenty, as never before, in the first scenes of most massively and avidly played games.

The second logic contributing to the present-day explosion of violence derives from wedding of their spectacularity to the cutting-edge, ratings- and profits-greedy media industry. Pictures and stories of violence are among the most sellable of the goods that industry puts on sale: the more cruel, gory and blood-curdling the better. No wonder that media managers love serving them how coffee-shop managers advertise the coffee they serve: fresh and hot. For the price of a gun, whoever wishes to make himself visible worldwide can count, without fail, on the impassioned and heart-felt cooperation of multi-billions-worth media; instantly, and with no further effort, one can raise even a relatively tiny and woefully parochial incident to the rank of a globally momentous, state-of-the-world-shattering event. Its echoes will reverberate for a long time to come – who knows, it might even be believed by the millions of viewers to be changing the course of history! Say what you will, this is an un-missable opportunity, a temptation that a budding terrorist worth his or her salt (as well as a downtrodden and dejected, demeaned and humiliated youngster drafted to the terrorist cause by its cunning and seasoned recruiters – the sole chance on offer) is utterly unlikely to overlook. Seekers of fame may rest assured that this society of ours, primed by liquidized evil and notorious for its inhospitality to nice and decent people, is unprecedentedly hospitable to Herostratus's heirs.

The two logics sketched briefly above are not, obviously, the *causes* of the repetitive, though scattered, explosions of 'floating violence'. Neither do they form, singly or together, its *sufficient condition*. But they constitute, when combined, its *necessary condition*. Without them both being present and acting in tandem, the outburst of violence in its present shape and form would've been all but inconceivable. And yet they are diligently excised from the most widely disseminated and believed interpretations of those explosions. Instead, we find references to '*religious* fundamentalism' and (after Huntington) 'clash of *civilizations*' as the culprits and defendants – as if evil was still, as of yore, solid, while its deregulation had not happened. What we face is the fallacy of taking form for substance, wrappings for contents, effects for causes – all in all, an interpretation for its object. It is high time to realize that the current rise in the volume and reach of violence needs to be seen against the background of a massive production of human misery: humiliation, denial of life prospects together with human dignity – and their only-to-be-expected outcome: a seething lust for vengeance. Terrorism, from which we need to expect still more to come, however eagerly governments pretend, and 'are seen on TV', to flex their muscles to tame and subdue it, is – we might say – the weapon of the collectively disarmed, a power of the individually disempowered. And it will remain such – as long as the agony and grief of having been excluded, or of living one's life under the threat of exclusion, go on rising unabated as at present. With this challenge to human dignity (rising even to our very survival) persisting, it would be naïve to the core to suppose that the seekers of conscripts to the suicide bombing squads will return from their recruiting hassle empty-handed – no matter what banner they propose for prospective suicide bombers to rally to.

It was Pope Francis who recently – alone of all the public figures in the global limelight – reached to the roots of our present predicament (in his Apostolic Exhortation *Evangelii Gaudium*), reminding us that it is a matter of hearing the 'cry of entire peoples', the poorest peoples of the earth, since 'peace is founded not only on respect for human rights, but also on respect for the rights of peoples':

59. Today in many places we hear a call for greater security. But until exclusion and inequality in society and between peoples are reversed, it will be impossible to eliminate violence. The poor and the poorer peoples are accused of violence, yet without equal opportunities the different forms of aggression and conflict will find a fertile terrain for growth and eventually explode. When a society – whether local, national or global – is willing to leave a part of itself on the fringes, no political programmes or resources spent on law enforcement or surveillance systems can indefinitely guarantee tranquility. This is not the case simply because inequality provokes a violent reaction from those excluded from the system, but because the socioeconomic system is unjust at its root. Just as goodness tends to spread, the toleration of evil, which is injustice, tends to expand its baneful influence and quietly to undermine any political and social system, no matter how solid it may appear. If every action has its consequences, an evil embedded in the structures of a society has a constant potential for disintegration and death. It is evil crystallized in unjust social structures, which cannot be the basis of hope for a better future. We are far from the so-called 'end of history', since the conditions for a sustainable and peaceful development have not yet been adequately articulated and realized.

60. Today's economic mechanisms promote inordinate consumption, yet it is evident that unbridled consumerism combined with inequality proves doubly damaging to the social fabric. Inequality eventually engenders a violence which recourse to arms cannot and never will be able to resolve. It serves only to offer false hopes to those clamouring for heightened security, even though nowadays we know that weapons and violence, rather than providing solutions, create new and more serious conflicts. Some simply content themselves with blaming the poor and the poorer countries themselves for their troubles; indulging in unwarranted generalizations, they claim that the solution is an 'education' that would tranquillize them, making them tame and harmless. All this becomes even more exasperating for the marginalized in the light of the widespread and deeply rooted corruption found in many countries – in their governments, businesses and institutions – whatever the political ideology of their leaders.

Pope Francis also pointed to the way – by no means easy, yet the only promising one – leading out of the evil and menacing condition in which we've cast ourselves by plugging our ears to that 'cry of entire peoples':

The need to resolve the structural causes of poverty cannot be delayed, not only for the pragmatic reason of its urgency for the good order of society, but because society needs to be cured of a sickness which is weakening and frustrating it, and which can only lead to new crises. Welfare projects, which meet certain urgent needs, should be considered merely temporary responses. As long as the problems of the poor are not radically resolved by rejecting the absolute autonomy of markets and financial speculation and by attacking the structural causes of inequality, no solution will be found for the world's problems or, for that matter, to any problems. Inequality is the root of social ills.

We can no longer trust in the unseen forces and the invisible hand of the market. Growth in justice requires more than economic growth, while presupposing such growth: it requires decisions, programmes, mechanisms and processes specifically geared to a better distribution of income, the creation of sources of employment and an integral promotion of the poor which goes beyond a simple welfare mentality. I am far from proposing an irresponsible populism, but the economy can no longer turn to remedies that are a new poison, such as attempting to increase profits by reducing the work force and thereby adding to the ranks of the excluded.

In the court of the present-day public opinion concerned with violence running out of control, the blame for the society that rejects – and, for all practical intents and purposes, makes null and void – the human, all too human, impulse of 'mutual aid and solidarity', is laid at the door of growing 'laicism and moral relativism', and away from its genuine causes, so vividly and lucidly described by Pope Francis. The sufferings of the demeaned, degraded, deprived and excluded victims could be 'extra-systemic': they might be strikingly similar, regardless of the specificity of the particular 'order' – and the 'discipline' it demands – by which they have been caused. The trick is how to use, fraudulently, the capital of human wrath and vengefulness stored by the wrongs committed by one 'system' against another in the on-going inter-systemic strife. The borders have already been pre-drawn by the apostles, priests and preachers of the antagonistic monotheisms; and as the great Norwegian anthropologist Fredrik Barth teaches, once the borders have been drawn, differences that justify drawing them are eagerly sought – and, of course, found, or invented. 'Their' (referring to people on the other side of the border) 'laicism and moral relativism', all but innocent of causing our rebellion-prompting misery, are among such 'differences' conveniently charged with responsibility for our anguish, and presented as the main (perhaps even the sole) obstacle to the restoration of justice, as well as of 'mutual aid and solidarity'.

Others accuse – and many others believe – on the contrary, that the rise and spread of religious fundamentalism are the ultimate causes of the present-day 'liquid violence'. Obviously, the religious variety of fundamentalism plays its role in channelling wrath and setting up targets for vengeance. There is a paradox endemic to a monotheist creed: it insists that the God of its choice is one and only – though by the very fact of persistently reiterating that assertion it obliquely admits the presence of that God's contenders. Because of that paradox, monotheistic religion cannot but be constantly ready for the fray – bristling with bayonets, combative and belligerent in confrontation with alternative (false, as it is bound to aver) pretenders to God's status. Monotheistic faith is, by its nature, militant and in a state of a permanent enmity and intermittent war – hot or cold – with the world outside its realm; it is viewed for that reason as a particularly tempting – indeed, the favourite – choice of motivation for warriors in a great variety of causes – especially the most intransigent and ruthless among them. After all, all the stops can be pulled out in a fight waged by those devoted to the Church in the name of the *one and only* God against His enemies. Once you know that, *in hoc signo vinces* – you can, and you will, catch as catch can. The popular, though questionable, quote from Dostoevsky suggests that 'If God does not exist, everything is permitted.' Closer to the facts of life – though, alas, even more portentous and, in its consequences, apocalyptic – is the conclusion that if there is one and only God, everything done in His name to His detractors, however cruel, goes. 'No doubt' equals 'no scruples'.

The principle of 'cuius regio eius religio', however, binds our no longer globalized and diasporized world. There are streets in densely populated London where Catholic and Protestant Churches, Sunnite and Shiite mosques, as well as orthodox and reform synagogues are erected just a few dozen yards from each other. Men and women of different faiths – heathens, heretics, dissenters or whatever other derogatory/stigmatizing/condemnatory names might be used to brand them – are no longer distant and misty creatures inhabiting seldom- or never-visited foreign lands, but next-door neighbours, work-mates, fathers and mothers of our children's school friends – at any rate, the daily, all-too-frequent sights on crowded city streets and squares. Mutual separation is no longer on the cards, however passionately we might try. Monotheistic gods are doomed to live in close proximity to each other on our incurably polytheistic planet; indeed, in each other's company. Huntington's vision of the war of civilization waged on a planetary scale does not descend to the urban level; at that level, as I have tried repeatedly to show, mixophilia gets the better of mixophobia. Willy-nilly, knowingly or not, by design or by default, ways and means of living daily in peace – even in collaboration – with difference are invented, experimented with, put to a test, and adopted. In one of his last oeuvres, Ulrich Beck noted the phenomenon of a 'God of one's own', the ongoing privatization of religious faith: indeed, a rising tendency to select/compose – individually, sometimes severally, and seldom collectively – the god to believe in and appeal to. Religious faith has been one of the many phenomena leaking down from institutions to individuals, from the 'Politics' with a capital 'p' to the sphere of individually run 'life politics'. The kind of evil it is most likely to encounter there is its liquid variety.

Let's turn to the last case in my sorely narrowed sample: our worries about the sustainability of the planet and the obstacles towering in the way of securing it against the tendency to devastate and exhaust its resources; the fear of impending catastrophe, which, crowded as we are inside an aircraft with the pilot's cabin empty, we feel hapless to prevent. The possibility of such a catastrophe is not a figment of our imagination. It has happened already in the past, even if not – as yet – on the global scale. One of the relatively well recorded cases is that of Easter Island, an isolated piece of land amidst the largest ocean on Earth (more than 2,000 km distant from the nearest land – the almost uninhabited Pitcairn Island – and more than 3,500 km from the South American continent), once self-sufficient and economically and culturally thriving from the time of the first human settlements established in the course of the first millennium, which, however, by the time of the European arrival in 1722 saw its population dropping to 2,000–3,000, from about 15,000 a mere century earlier.[14] The main culprit and immediate cause of that catastrophe was overharvesting and overhunting, resulting in deforestation of the island, followed in turn by erosion of the topsoil. In the light of the data one could collate from all parts of the globe, the sad fate of Easter Island may well be viewed as a local rehearsal for a forthcoming global production of the drama.

In his new book, Arne Johan Vetlesen, a remarkable Norwegian philosopher, confronts point-blank the task of 'further reflection on the gravity of current dangers'; doing so, he strengthens yet more your case, reaching to the roots of the present trouble by pointing out that 'the longer nature is treated as a mere means to human-centred ends, the more degraded it will become. And the more degraded nature becomes, the more of an uphill struggle it will be to make the argument – however impressive in theory – that nature possesses intrinsic value.'[15] We have landed in a sort of a vicious circle. Short of a radical reversal of trend and profound revision of our hegemonic philosophy and mode of life, we are confronted with a challenge no less daunting and arduous than the untying of the proverbial Gordian knot. It has happened, and continues to happen, that, in a stark opposition to popular hopes, the departures in scientific knowledge and technological know-how which we dub summarily 'progress' are undercutting the very conditions required for human collective survival. As Vetlesen puts it:

> The less there actually exists of nature *qua* unexplored, unknown, unexploited, the more the cosmologies fashioned by the sense of powerlessness come to lose their hold. The shift, then, is from being at the mercy of nature and all the nonhuman life-forms and species it consists of, to commanding what demonstrably is increasingly growing control and mastery over it, principally by way of a wave of new technologies immensely more efficient than those predating them. '*Extractivism*' is Naomi Klein's apt term for the still dominant paradigm: 'a nonreciprocal, dominance-based relationship with the earth, one purely of taking'...working *against* rather than with the flow, rhythms, and regenerational dynamics and capacities of nature.[16]

And then Vetlesen quotes Teresa Brennan:

> Capital plays God and redirects nature at its own speed and from its own subject-centred standpoint. It is playing with high stakes here, because it is literally altering the *physis* of the world, adjusting the inbuilt logic of nature and the spatio-temporal continuum to suit itself. [...] It establishes its own foundation, but it does so by consuming the real foundations, the logic of natural substances.[17]

Brennan and her contemporaries had their predecessors – the most noteworthy and perhaps the most influential among them having been Lewis Mumford.[18] Well before the current explosion of 'sustainability' concerns and studies, even before the very concept of the 'sustainability of the planet' was coined, Mumford elaborated two ideal-typical attitudes to non-human nature and their underlying philosophies, related respectively to agriculture (confined to its pre-industrialization history) and mining (in the form coming to full maturity in the middle of the nineteenth century):

> Agriculture creates balance between wild nature and man's social needs. It returns deliberately what man subtracts from the earth; while the ploughed field, the trim orchard, the serried vineyard, the

vegetables, the grains, the flowers, are all examples of disciplined purpose, orderly growth, and beautiful form. The process of mining, on the other hand, is destructive: the immediate product of mining is disorganized and inorganic; and what is once taken out of the quarry or the pithead cannot be replaced. Add to this the fact that continuing occupation in agriculture brings cumulative improvement of the landscape and a finer adaptation of it to human needs; while mines as a rule pass quickly from riches to exhaustion, from exhaustion to desertion, often within a few generations. Mining thus presents the very image of human discontinuity, here today and gone tomorrow, now feverish with gain, now depleted and vacant.[19]

In our age lived under the rule of technology developing its own developmental logic and own momentum, the earth, as Martin Heidegger noted, reveals itself as (only) a coal mining district, its soil as a mineral deposit:

The windmill does not unlock energy from the air currents in order to store it. In contrast, a tract of land is challenged into the putting out of coal and ore. The earth now reveals itself as a coal mining district, the soil as a mineral deposit. The field that the peasant formerly cultivated and set in order [bestellte] appears differently than it did when to set in order still meant to take care of and to maintain. The work of the peasant does not challenge the soil of the field. In the sowing of the grain it places the seed in the keeping of the forces of growth and watches over its increase.[20]

So we have a strong case – but so did all those authors quoted above, as well as lots of others here unnamed, though many of them are recognized as reputable and widely read. The facts speak for themselves, and the conclusions are thoroughly convincing; but there are scarcely any (or at least far too few) signs of them being given the attention which their import and gravity require. We may recently have talked and written more than before about the dangers that threaten the sustainability of our planet, and so also about the prospects for our collective survival. But our conduct and its accomplishments did not match the words – however many of us were addressed and at whatever level of power and influence they were pronounced; this also, in itself, is a manifestation of the 'liquidity' of evil. Our collective consciousness must yet – so it seems – cover a lot of distance in order to reach our collective conscience, and through it beget an adequate collective action. We may talk and think differently from how we did a few decades ago, but our way of daily life, and our hierarchy of preferences in particular, have hardly twitched – if anything, their ominous, doomful proclivities have acquired their own self-reinforcing momentum.

In 1975–6, Elias Canetti collected a number of his essays, written within a 26-year time span, in a volume entitled *Das Gewissen der Worte* '(Conscience of Words)'; the volume closes with the speech on the writing profession, delivered by Canetti in January 1976 in Munich. In it, he confronts the question whether, in the present world situation, 'there is something to which writers or people heretofore thought to be writers could be of use'. To explain what sort of a writer he has in mind, he quotes a statement made by an unknown author on 23 August 1939: 'It's over. Were I a real writer, I should've been able to prevent the war'; the author of these words insists that a writer is 'real' inasmuch as her or his words make a difference between well-being and catastrophe. What makes writers 'real' is the impact of their words on reality – in Canetti's rendition, the 'desire to assume responsibility for everything that can be expressed in words, and to do penance for their, the words', failure'. To leave no room for his opinion to be taken lightly as referring to grave, yet fortunately past events, he emphasizes that the menace has lost nothing of its topicality: 'there are no writers today, but we ought to passionately desire that there be...In a world, which one would most willingly define as the blindest of worlds, the presence of people who nevertheless insist on the possibility of its change acquires supreme importance.'

Our world seems be anything but hospitable to 'real writers' as described by Canetti. It appears to be well protected not against catastrophes, but against their few-and-far-between prophets, while most of us, the residents of that well-protected world, are well protected against listening to the few voices crying in their respective wildernesses – at least as long as the right to residence is not yet brusquely denied us, as it is bound to be in a not-so-distant future if our contrived deafness persists. As another great intellectual of yore, Arthur Koestler, kept reminding us on the eve of another catastrophe, 'in 1933 and during the next two or three years, the only people with an intimate understanding of what

went on in the young Third Reich were a few thousand refugees',
a distinction that condemned them to the 'always unpopular,
shrill-voiced part of Cassandra'. Koestler's own conclusion was
sombre: 'Amos, Hosea, Jeremiah, were pretty good propagandists,
and yet failed to shake their people and to warn them. Cassandra's
voice was said to have pierced walls, and yet the Trojan war took
place.' It seems that one needs catastrophes to happen in order to
recognize and admit their coming. A chilling thought, if there ever
was one...

Please allow me now to turn to another issue you've raised and
presented with exquisite clarity – that of adiaphorization, a phenomenon also closely related to the 'liquidity' of the contemporary
evils, and bearing part of the responsibility for its 'liquidization':
a matter tremendously relevant to the phenomenal assiduity and
staying power of evil now, as much – or perhaps yet more – than
it was in the earlier, 'solid' phases of the modern era. I can add
little to your succinct, yet all the same comprehensive and exhaustive, account. Just one point: 'Adiaphorization' is aimed at and
results in axiological neutralization – 'adiaphora' are value-neutral
thoughts and deeds exempted from evaluation (particularly in
religious or ethical terms) and thereby cast outside the universe of
religious and moral obligations; in dealing with adiaphoric objects,
inanimate and animate alike, moral impulses are put to sleep
nevertheless of the ethical load of the consequences of action or
a refusal to act. This is true now as it was then – when the term
was coined and deployed in the resolutions of Church councils. I
am inclined to suggest, however, that in modern times adiaphorization has acquired an additional meaning and application. On
top of announcing value-neutrality, it takes in exclusion/elimination
on the ground of irrelevance: unimportance to the results of
planned action, inability to contribute to its success as much as to
its failure, and thus an absence of instrumental value – and, all in
all, inutility. Adiaphorized objects are in such cases a waste of
instrumental rationality and rational calculation – not so much
resented or hated as simply unnoted and left out of account. They
are not taken in consideration when policies are designed; they
are relegated to the category of '*collateral* victims' of campaigns
and policies – objects whose pains and sufferings are not included
in the costs of the undertaking and not factored in when the cost-
to-effects ratio is forecast or appraised. They fall victims of *neglect*

arising from disinterestedness and indifference, rather than of explicit or unwitting aversion, deprecation or hostility – though the latter, time and again, tend to be manufactured after the fact and invoked in argument once the outcomes of negligence are stamped and publicly censured. Exclusion, or the prospect and sanction of exclusion, on the ground of uselessness grows nowadays in its spread and gathers momentum. I suggest that it is on course to leave behind and dwarf other manifestations of evil. It tends to become evil's *principal playground*, and evil's most widely and commonly deployed *weapon*.

What all this argument amounts to is that liquid evil is not an operable cancer tumour that can be separated from healthy tissue and removed while leaving the rest of social organism unscathed. It is an endemic part of that organism, indispensable for its normal functioning and survival in its present form. Evil may be trimmed, pared and contracted, and indeed it needs to be resisted and fought back whenever encountered, but it cannot be cut out completely. Evil is built into our common mode of being-in-the-world, the world which we inhabit and share. Elimination of evil, if at all conceivable, requires no less than a thorough rethinking and radical overhaul of this mode.

LD   The unholy trinity of the core components of liquid evil – deregulation, dissemination and privatization, which you describe as 'liquidization' of evil – is quite close to what we may well call the tyranny of an economy inseparable from rational impersonalism, which I am going to mention here.

Home is a painful problem for an ambitious and creative individual, but not for that tyranny of the economy which we euphemistically refer to as one world. A curious philosophical book, disguised as an innocent fable and published at the beginning of the eighteenth century, may throw new light on all these entanglements and the mixed logic of modernity. The book is Bernard Mandeville's *Fable of the Bees: Private Vices, Publick Benefits* (two successive editions in 1714 and 1723). Originating in 1705 as a sixpenny satire in verse titled *The Grumbling Hive; or, Knaves Turn'd Honest*, it later developed into a book through the addition of 'Remarks' and other pieces.

A witty and subtle attack against three vices, Fraud, Luxury and Pride, the poem offered a strong argument, presenting a hive as a mirror of human society. Like society, the hive lives in corruption and prosperity. Yet it feels nostalgia for virtue and keeps praying to recover it. When the prayer is granted, everything changes overnight beyond recognition. There is no more vice, but activity and prosperity disappear. What replaces activity and prosperity are sloth, poverty and boredom. Last but not least, all this happens in a considerably reduced population.

The essence of what I would define as Mandeville's paradox is that individual vice in universalistic morality can turn into a public benefit, whereas individual virtue does not necessarily increase the well-being of society. Once society can benefit from our pursuit of our own interest, we cannot lightly dismiss private vices. Mandeville achieves something similar to Machiavelli's view: no one single truth exists in social reality, and every coin has two sides as far as human interaction and social life are concerned. Nothing personal lurks behind the predominant social and moral order, and nobody can be blamed in person for the shortcomings and imperfections of our life. Our jealousy and greed just happen to coincide with other individuals' wishes and desires.

Public benefits result from private vices just as common good comes from our realism, sober-mindedness and imperfection. Nothing is certain and obvious here. A greedy but laborious fool can be more useful for society than an idle sage – in this, we can clearly hear the early voice of modernity with its ambivalence, scepticism and relativism.

What can be found behind the fictional paraphernalia of Mandeville's *Fable of the Bees* is Pierre Bayle's *Dictionnaire historique et critique* (1697). Mandeville's scepticism, antirationalism, relativism, along with a strong emphasis on psychology and sensualism, link him to the French theoretical and intellectual influences of Bayle and Pierre Gassendi. Incidentally, Adam Smith knew this fable through Francis Hutcheson. The following well-known expression of Smith's really has much in common with the intrinsic logic of Mandeville's paradox: 'It is not from the benevolence of the butcher, the brewer, or the baker that we expect our dinner, but from their regard to their own interest.'[21]

Here we can hear the birth-cry of 'rational impersonalism', as Ken Jowitt called it.[22] Impersonalism, ambiguity and ambivalence, coupled with what Max Weber once described as 'the iron cage', are those intrinsic forces that make modernity, and capitalism in particular, so deplorable and hateful in the eyes of those who want to restore what has been irreversibly lost by our modern world – namely, the predictability, clarity, visibility, stability and certainty of social reality; safety and security; political passions and social upheavals; emotional intimacy; human fellowship; a sense of community.

Yet this is all but one side of the coin. The celebration of rational impersonalism and our private vices turned into public benefits reflected the uncritical and unreflective attitude of a post-communist society. Mandeville's fable of the bees seems to have been an almost-perfect allegory for a transitory period in a society where economic and moral individualism was long suppressed and then released with no way to counterbalance the portrayal both of self and of the world around oneself in black and white. A gradual destruction of the public domain, without which democratic politics becomes impossible, was not on the minds and lips of those who celebrated the free market and the invisible hand as just different words for democracy.

Jeffrey Sommers and Charles Woolfson's book *The Contradictions of Austerity: The Socio-Economic Costs of the Neoliberal Baltic Model* is a timely, incisive, perceptive, provocative and important book which addresses all these issues. Hit by the economic crisis with all its devastating effects, the Baltic States underwent similar processes in tackling nearly the same challenges – yet their responses were far from identical. Whereas Latvia got a loan from the International Monetary Fund (IMF), Lithuania firmly refused to do so, and claimed credit for overcoming the crisis with no external assistance. Without further ado, let us take a look at some side-effects of Lithuania's austerity policy.

Drastic cuts in public spending – no matter how indispensable and unavoidable – resulted in a rapid deterioration of the public domain. Although Lithuanian political commentators and opinion makers, like their other Baltic colleagues, often stressed the need to oppose Russia's propaganda and information war, the weakening of higher-quality and investigative journalism, smaller publishers, civic education and translation programmes hardly served the purpose of strengthening the public domain and civil society in the Baltic States. That analytical journalism, political analysis, high-brow and non-commercial sectors of culture suffered tremendously from austerity is too obvious a fact to be challenged. One of the biggest contradictions and paradoxes of austerity policies in the Baltic States was the ever-growing dependence of the Baltic region on Russian media and information. Contrary to the widespread opinion that a fast recovery from the crisis, at any cost, would leave Lithuania stronger vis-à-vis Russia and its increasingly aggressive geopolitics, civil society and solidarity scarcely benefited from the aforementioned drastic cuts and austerity policies in general.

Yet the editors and contributors in the book in question go even further. They argue that the paradigm of austerity in our economics and politics would have been unable to harm the public sector if the Baltic region had been less dependent on the neoliberal model. The ambivalence of the major narratives of modern economics and politics is too obvious to need emphasis. Like the *Fable of the Bees*, the story of austerity reads like an exciting tale of wisdom and virtue. As James K. Galbraith writes in the Foreword to the book: 'Whereas the tale of expansionary austerity is simple, timeless, and context-free – an allegory of virtue rewarded – the tapestry presented in these pages could not have been woven in any other time or place.'[23]

As for the wisdom of the classics of economic thought, it is more relevant than ever before, since the founding fathers of socialism and liberalism warned us long ago against the excesses and dark side of modernity. Summing up the rich analytic tapestry of the book in the Conclusion, which focuses on the neoliberal Baltic austerity model as opposed to Social Europe based on solidarity, the editors of the book, Jeffrey Sommers and Charles Woolfson, note: 'Undreamed of only a decade ago, many Europeans have experienced the widespread return of what Karl Marx described as "immiseration" and ignoring Adam Smith's caution that "no society can surely be flourishing and happy, of which the far greater part of the members are poor and miserable".'[24]

According to Galbraith, the austerity dogma found the Baltic States an almost perfect place in which to carry out a dangerous social experiment of this sort: 'It is the fate of small countries to serve as pilot projects, as battlegrounds, and as the point-of-origin for myths.'[25] Contrary to the Keynesian paradigm of stimulation of the public sector and spending, or the Schumpeterian paradigm of innovation as the very core of the economy and as the bridge between the private and the public, the austerity paradigm, with its zero respect for any sort of regulation, public safety and well-being, coupled with neoliberal deregulatory zeal, produced a frightening degree of indifference to the public domain, education and culture. Small wonder, then, that Charles Woolfson and Arunas Juska offer a polemical postscript to this book, which focuses on the tragic collapse of the roof of the Lithuanian-owned Maxima supermarket in Riga on 21 November 2013. This prompts their grim sum-up of the story: 'The Maxima episode reveals criminogenic characteristics of a new capitalism that developed in the Baltic region following the collapse of the Soviet Union.'[26]

The question arises here of whether the Baltic States could have avoided this dangerous – not to say devastating – social experiment. The premise of several contributors to the book is quite clear on this: due to their being in a boundary region between Russia and Germany (and close to the Nordic countries), the burden of their history, their complex political and historical legacy, existential threats from Russia, completely discredited left-wing values, the ideological rejection of socialism, and the duality of money flowing in and people moving out, the Baltic States were tailor-made for this civilizational experiment. 'Each of these countries has been heavily funded by private capital inflow and official European assistance. Each is dealing with a rapid decline of population and emigration of educated and able-bodied workers. In each, the political classes disregarded warning signs and forged ahead, committing themselves irrevocably to the austerian dogma.'[27]

Could the Baltics have come up with an alternative scenario relying on classical economic recipes for recovery? Or was there any other option for them, in their attempt to catch up with the EU and to avoid joining the league of those unfortunate actors in Eastern Europe that found themselves on the losing side of the game? Serious doubts arise here, as the Baltic States had to tackle the problem of their underdevelopment. They had to speed up the process of integration at any cost. Hence what Erik S. Reinert and Rainer Kattel describe as a 'failed and asymmetrical integration'. They suggest that 'despite impressive growth numbers in exports and foreign direct investments, Eastern European economies failed to develop genuine Schumpeterian dynamics of imperfect competition', with all its preconditions and implications for the free-market economy.[28]

The themes of a Latin-Americanization of European integration and underdevelopment are echoed by Michael Hudson who stresses the structural underdevelopment of Latvia created by independence. Arguing with neoliberals who claim that austerity could restore Latvia's economic growth, Hudson notes that Latvia's 'economic contraction in 2008–10 was brutal' and that 'it remains the most impoverished country in the EU after Romania and Bulgaria'.[29] Introducing the book, Jeffrey Sommers and Charles Woolfson subscribe to this point of view, adding to the topic of integration-through-austerity that 'the Baltics' economic plunge was purely a result of the private-sector banking crisis, which in the context of the global recession revealed the deeper structural underdevelopment of their respective economies. These uncomfortable truths have been obscured in the haste to discover a generalized formula for the successful imposition of austerity measures in the Baltic States.'[30]

To cut a convoluted story short, the question arises here of whether the Baltic recovery was a success story. Here is Galbraith's sombre and sobering answer:

> And of course, a common theme here is that the Baltic success is no success at all. Rising gross domestic product (GDP) is a benefit only to those whose own incomes are actually rising, and many are not. The Baltics have become polarized and segmented societies, dominated by oligarchs and civil servants, with low wages, paltry benefits, and precariousness for the rest. It is a tale of life rendered so uncompromising – by ideology, by oligarchs, by creditors, by economists – that many in each country are leaving. Many do not expect ever to return. All three countries are in rapid demographic decline, which if it continues will soon enough transform them into retirement communities, supported largely by remittances, for so long as they last.[31]

Here comes an existential challenge to the Baltic countries, especially Lithuania and Latvia. Over the past ten years, more than half a million people – in most cases, highly qualified, educated, active and civic-minded individuals – have left Lithuania. The country's population has decreased quite drastically, and it is now below 3 million people, even though this first rebellious republic to break away from the former USSR met its independence with a population of 3.5 million. Much ink has been spilled in arguing whether this reflects the general twentieth-century pattern of social mobility in a small nation with a large diaspora, or whether it was the outcome of a new bad state, lacking competence in all too many areas of modern life.

In addition to Chicago, Illinois, in the USA – which has for a long time been described by émigrés and local Lithuanians alike as another Lithuania outside of Lithuania – cities in the EU like Dublin and London have become the new little Lithuanias over the past years. The Lithuanian writer Marius Ivaškevičius penned the play *Expulsion* (2011) in which he depicted the lives, passions and dramas of economic migrants from Lithuania, Latvia and other Eastern European countries, in London. This play has recently been staged by the Lithuanian theatre director Oskaras Koršunovas in Vilnius and Riga, where it became a sensational cult production. His is a new Lithuanian – and, perhaps, Baltic – narrative: a postmodern epic of a society trying to cope with and swamped by change, and a great saga of the new *austeriat*, as these people are referred to in the book edited by Sommers and Woolfson. Where social theorists spoke before of the *precariat* (Guy Standing and yourself, Zygmunt), the *austeriat* now appears as the local-turned-global segment of alienated labour and mass impoverishment.[32]

In fact, Eastern European countries seem to be stuck mentally somewhere between the discovery of the intrinsic logic of capitalism characteristic of the nineteenth century and post-Weimar-Republic period – an incredibly fast economic growth and a passionate advocacy of the values of free enterprise and capitalism, accompanied by a good deal of anomie, fission of the body social, stark divisions in society, shocking degree of corruption, culture of poverty (to recall Oscar Lewis's term, referring to low trust, self-victimization, disbelief in social ties and networks, contempt for institutions, etc.) – and cynicism.

As Galbraith sums it up, offering a metaphor of the Devil's bargain in our accelerated history and politics:

Still, one can't help but wonder. Suppose Mephistopheles had appeared before the Baltic independence leaders in 1991 and had offered this bargain: Independence. Capitalism. Freedom. Democracy. The dissolution of the USSR. NATO. Europe. And eventually the euro. And the price? Only that within a half century the Latvians, Lithuanians, and Estonians would be an elderly remnant in their own countries, their society in tatters, their children in economic exile, their homes abandoned or in hock, and eventually their economies and governments permanently subordinated to new elites – local and foreign.

Would they have taken the deal?[33]

What is this all about? Is it about the Devil in economics and politics? Or moral blindness? Or our being unable to see and grasp the world around us other than through the pleasure- and profit-maximizing lenses that reduce the human being to a statistic and relegate his or her suffering to the margins of the GDP? I guess everything is less melodramatic and more related to the unbearable lightness of incessant change.

Our postmodern and post-totalitarian era, in the Baltic region, proved capable of squeezing two centuries of uninterrupted European history into one decade of 'transition' of the Baltic States and other East-Central European countries from the planned economy of communism to the free-market economy and global capitalism. In a way, Eastern Europe appears to have become a kind of laboratory, where the speed of social change and cultural transformation could be measured and tested. In fact, the Baltic countries and their societies are far ahead of what we know as the grand historical narrative, or, put bluntly, predictable and moralizing history – indeed, these societies are faster than history.

Yet, keeping in mind what is happening now in Russia, the question is quite simple: did the Baltic States have a plausible alternative in squeezing the generations- or century-long developments of the West into the decade or two offered for them to catch up, other than through the neoliberal model? I am not convinced that they did. Of course, this remark does not diminish the value of an excellent volume with the charms of its alternative, or imagined, history, and questions like, say, 'What would have happened had this or that been so?'

The Baltics paid the price for their indispensable and unavoidable acceleration of history and development. The alternatives could have led them back to the East, instead of the West, as we now clearly see. *C'est tout.*

ZB   I fully understand why you focus your analysis so closely on the plight of Lithuania and the experience of Lithuanians (in both meanings of 'experience': *Erfahrung* – 'what happened to me' – and *Erlebnis* – 'how it felt'), as well as on their responses to ensuing challenges; Lithuania is indeed a case of its own (as is any other country, as a matter of fact), but there are features strikingly common in many other cases – a circumstance which prompts us to shift the search for their sources to phenomena beyond local idiosyncrasies. A while ago I was asked by the editors of *Eutopia* – an Italian-based monthly, but all-European in its selection of authors and audience – to comment on the twenty-fifth anniversary of the fall of the Berlin Wall. In reply, I turned to the Polish plight/experience and the Poles' responses, which, it appears, are very much akin to what you have observed in Lithuania. Let me quote from my reply:

> In the 24 October issue of *Gazeta Wyborcza*, a leading opinion-making daily in that country, its cultural editor Roman Pawłowski suggests the co-presence of two generations into which the present-day Poles are split; he dubs them, respectively, 'children of the transformation' and 'children of crisis'. The first of the two named generations, now in their forties and above, 'came to believe, on the tide of the enthusiasm of the 90s, that "education and hard work will bring a decent life", [but now] drudge 16 hours a day, allowing the corporations, for the sake of repaying credit and sustaining the family, to mistreat and abuse them'. Members of the other generation, now in their 30s, who 'have no families and not being credit-worthy have no credit to repay, toil in rubbish jobs and live in rented rooms or are stuck in the parental home'. The members of the first generation, as Pawłowski suggests, nevertheless still believe 'in the superiority of private ownership over public and of the individual over public interest, are suspicious of public expenditures which they view as "throwing money away", while viewing the beneficiaries of public assistance [...] as spongers'. 'What counts for them is their own comfort and interest – it is they, after all, who pay taxes and contribute to the GDP.' Members of the younger generation differ: they 'have no illusions as to the [merits] of global markets' – while things shared and public are to them 'as important as individual and private matters'. The growth of GDP does not particularly concern them – they are more concerned with social capital. 'Though their attitude to the world is also selfish, they see no problem with helping the weaker, aware that they themselves may well find themselves in need of similar help.'

I believe moreover that the net meant to catch the goings-on and their causes needs to be cast yet wider than the areas of Lithuania and Poland – close geographical neighbours, side by side. I started my comments for *Eutopia* by observing that 'A spectre hovers over the ruins of the Berlin Wall: the spectre of no alternative.'

'Impersonalism, ambiguity, and ambivalence', 'destruction of the public domain', 'the widespread return of what Karl Marx described as "immiseration"': your inventory of ills (at least pan-European, if not all-planetary) that haunt the world stripped of a tangible alternative to itself is exhaustive and precise. Never before has Cornelius Castoriadis's observation that what was wrong with our society was that it stopped questioning itself sounded more convincing, definite and, indeed, unquestionable as it does today.

This does not mean, of course, that we've stopped complaining about the sorry state of our personal affairs. And no wonder, considering that few of us may count on escaping the threat of being cast, time and again, on the receiving side of the inhuman, alienating callousness of ambient impersonality, insensitivity, lack of compassion that you spot in the mood of our times of which you write. If we wished to record the grievances (all of them – from mere gripe, through grumbling, and all the way to pugnacious defiance), made audible thanks to the unheard-of numbers of unprecedentedly efficient broadcasting contraptions, we would need a genuinely infinite supply of *cahiers de doléance* of the type allegedly instrumental in precipitating the French Revolution of 1789. Disaffections and dissatisfactions, multifarious as they are – but hardly ever short of (valid and, all too often, convincing) reasons – are a most salient characteristic of the public mood and the perpetual, incessant talk of the town.

What it does mean, however, is the political ineffectuality of discontent and protestations. Once potent weapons of collective political action, of self-assertion and change, they have been recycled into prime lubricants of the consumerist economy's flywheel. The effects of the banes for which our post-liberal consumerist society is notorious tend to be suffered individually and individually groused about and sulked over; equally individual, personal and private tend to be the sought-after life-jackets and life-boats. The short-circuiting of adversities and hardships perceived and lived through as cases of personal misfortune takes the form best described as an 'explosive' or 'carnival-style' manifestation of contestant solidarity: of, as a rule, ad hoc, short-lived coalitions of contradictory and competitive interests, resistant to blending and gelling into sustained political movements armed with collective visions of reform and a cohesive programme of concerted action. Conflicts of interest are merely temporarily suspended or glossed over; attempts to confront them head-on, not to mention their serious negotiation, lead momentarily to discord, bickering and dissolution.

A common denominator most likely to emerge victorious from the competition of various adhesives haggled about on that Kuwaiti-bazaar-like reincarnation of the *agora* – an adhesive advertised as certain to hold together those endemically frail and fissiparous, ad hoc coalitions – is the typically consumerist interest in more money for more purchases; the mantra of rising consumption which passes for a universal recipe for happiness and satisfaction with life constitutes, after all, the 'hegemonic philosophy' of the present times: a mind-set that stands the biggest chance of the widest, cross-class and cross-culture, support. The consumerist economy, complete with the consumerist mentality it spawns – the genuine meta-cause of variegated individual discontents – emerges from the periodic carnival-style explosions of ambient dissatisfaction that has condensed into public anger not only intact and unscathed, but re-asserted and indeed reinforced. As was long ago explained by Mikhail Bakhtin, one (perhaps the paramount) of carnival's functions is therapy of the ailing status quo; in their role as safety valves of sorts, carnivals allow periodic release of pent-up resentment against whatever currently passes for the 'public arena' and its impact on individual capabilities – and so allow the participants to return to the annoying and incapacitating daily routine with replenished reserves of endurance capacity. Carnivals of public resentment and manifestations of dissent perform the task of the socio-political replica of health farms, which the socio-political system needs regularly to visit in order to purge itself, for the time being, of potentially toxic fluids generated and stored by the hardships of the day-in, day-out competition, rivalry and exercises in one-upmanship it necessitates, and of the fears of degradation, demotion and exclusion which it inevitably creates.

The consumerist economy is aided and abetted by the hegemony of the philosophy of 'wellness' ('Being a good person these days does not mean curbing the sinful longings of the body...it means living well', as Hervé Juvin put it in *The Coming of the Body*, as quoted by Carl Cederström and André Spicer;[34] 'Today, wellness has become a moral demand – about which we are constantly and tirelessly reminded', they themselves suggest: 'The ideological element of wellness is particularly visible' in 'those who fail to look after their bodies [being] demonised as lazy, feeble and weak willed'; 'When health becomes an ideology, the failure to conform becomes a stigma'[35] – indeed: no ideology is complete without appointing and stigmatizing its infidels, heretics, detractors and saboteurs) – only together do they form a 'a web-like network of capillaries, embedded in tissue, connecting them'.[36] Capillary vessels penetrate, impregnate, saturate the whole organism, being, as they are, 'only one epithelial cell thick. They are so thin that blood cells can only pass through them in single file.' In its liquidized condition, we may say, evil fills the 'web-like network of capillaries' of the society of individualized, self-centred and wellness-obsessed – after the pattern of Rabelais's Abbey of Thélème – consumers. But we may also observe that the particular liquid filling and conducted by the capillary vessels of such a society is of a kind that generates effects of leukaemia instead of a normal blood circulation.

According to the state-of-the-art scholarly opinion, 'people with leukaemia produce abnormal white blood cells. These abnormal cells accumulate in the bone marrow and prevent the production of other important blood cells. Most of the problems associated with leukaemia are caused by the lack of normal cells in the blood, rather than the leukaemia cells themselves'; 'Leukaemia cells can collect in many different tissues and organs, such as the digestive tract, kidneys, lungs, lymph nodes, or other parts of the body, including the eyes, brain, and testicles.' The particularly treacherous trait of leukaemia consists in covering its tracks until the normal function of blood circulation (that is, the function of distributing the 'oxygenated blood from arteries to the tissues of the body and to feed deoxygenated blood from the tissues back into the veins'[37]) is reversed: 'When symptoms appear, they generally are mild at first and gradually get worse, but sometimes they don't worsen until many years after an initial diagnosis.'[38]

To make things worse still, as long as they stay mild and stop short of turning (imperceptibly) into a compulsion or addiction, perceived and experienced as a sort of second and greatly improved nature, the 'mild symptoms' may feel unambiguously pleasurable, mixing gratifying (and therefore pleasing) sensual enthralments with the self-flattering sense of a well-performed duty (duty to oneself – raised to the rank of the social, indeed the human, duty). Cederström and Spicer quote from Alenka Zupančič's *The Odd One In*: 'There is a spectacular rise of what we might call a bio-morality (as well as morality of feelings and emotions), which promotes the following fundamental axiom: a person who feels good (and is happy) is a good person; a person who feels bad is a bad person".'[39]

What casts and holds evil in that form of liquid – capillary, and ultimately leukaemic – condition is, in the last resort, the so-called 'individualization process', which boils down in practice to the privatization of concerns and obligations deriving from the challenges of human existence. As Isabell Lorey crisply put it:

> This leads to a form of governing that at least since Thomas Hobbes has been viewed as no longer possible: a government that is not legitimized by promising protection and security. Contrary to the old rule of a domination that demands obedience in exchange for protection, neoliberal governing proceeds primarily through social insecurity, through regulating the minimum of assurance while simultaneously increasing instability. In the course of the dismantling and remodelling of the welfare state and the rights associated with it, a form of government is established that is based on the greatest possible insecurity, promoted by proclaiming the alleged absence of alternatives.[40]

And let me add, by courtesy of this fateful transformation in the strategy of domination and governance, liquidization of evil no longer needs legitimation; for all practical intents and purposes, it has become a condition by which we are all constituted and in whose perpetual reproduction we are all (by design or by default, willingly or unwittingly – having been caught off-guard) drawn upon and engaged. In the thoroughly individualized (in the sense spelt-out above) society, reproduction of 'liquid evil' is a DIY job jointly performed by us as individuals – with the role of governments reduced to that of enabling us, boosting and compelling us, to do that job, and do it properly. To quote another of Lorey's succinct summaries: 'the state increasingly limits itself to discourses and practices of police and military safeguarding, which in turn increasingly operate with disciplinary control and surveillance techniques...the more social safeguards are minimized, and the more precarization increases, the more there is a battle to maximize domestic security'.[41]

In short, the preconditions for the present-day liquidity of evil – the ubiquity of evil-conducting capillary vessels and the density of their network – are closely correlated with the present-day government-promoted normalization of social/existential insecurity. 'There is a sense of overwhelming precariousness, in work, in matters of money, and in culture generally; a feeling of being kept in suspense which appears as like a law of nature, rather than something human-made' – is how Ivor Southwood summed up our shared condition a few years ago.[42] He proceeded by arguing, utterly convincingly, that 'this state of insecurity – which taps into our deepest fears and desires, much as neurosis draws on and distorts the unconscious – is artificially maintained, while being presented as inevitable, just a fact of life'. Under such conditions, even the 'meagre business of keeping afloat' demands a 'sink-or-swim individualism'.[43] Political and commercial interests are, of course, only too eager to draw benefits from those conditions: a nearly total submission of one's time and energy (indeed, the well-nigh totality of one's life pursuits) can be sweetened, rendered seductive and offered for consumption by being presented as the act of total liberation.

2

From the Kafkaesque to the Orwellesque?

War Is Peace, and Peace Is War

Leonidas Donskis   The drama of Russia and Ukraine now dominates public attention in the EU, and rightly so. Yet I would approach this tragedy from a slightly different perspective from that offered by the majority of commentators. Before I turn to the Orwellesque world of Putinism and new aggression, I will try to expose the venomous role of the intelligentsia and spin doctors within it.

The extreme power of manipulation, in terms of public opinion and imagology, and its political and moral implications are well revealed by one film that has contributed to the critique of today's controlling political structures. This is Barry Levinson's film *Wag the Dog*. The film tells us the story of Hollywood producer Stanley Motss and the Washington spin doctor Conrad Brean, who are supposed to save the White House when the President has a scandalous affair.

The duet of Dustin Hoffman and Robert De Niro reveals with skill a world of people who are talented but also amoral and value-disoriented. Yet the portrayal of instrumental mind and instrumental morality is not the only merit of this great film. Created in 1997, it concerned a military campaign in Yugoslavia (although the film mentions Albania) during the height of Bill Clinton and Monica Lewinsky's sex scandal. Of course, it would be silly to claim, with any seriousness, that the war in Yugoslavia was required because of US domestic politics, and as a means of smothering the scandal. 'Pacifist' Western Europe wanted this war perhaps even more than 'militaristic' America. The USA was the wand that was used to solve the problem.

But this film leaves an impression due to its emphasis on something else: it just so happens that a war can be fabricated – in the same way, it turns out, that one might direct public opinion with the intention that a war would be wanted, or even greatly desired. Create an artificial crisis, sacrifice a few dozen innocent lives to a political Moloch, increase people's sense of insecurity – and, everyone, in a flash, almost overnight, will want both a firm controlling hand, tough rhetoric and, perhaps, even war: in short, something similar to being beyond good and evil.

In fact, the film in question predicted something even more dangerous and sinister than it was able to articulate and address in the lines of its characters' monologues and dialogues. In the contemporary world, manipulation by political advertisement is capable not only of creating people's needs and their criteria for happiness, but also of fabricating the heroes of our time and controlling the imagination of the masses through laudatory biographies and success stories. These abilities make one pause for thought about a 'velvet' totalitarianism – a controlled form of manipulating consciousness and imagination that is cloaked as liberal democracy, which allows the enslavement and control even of its critics.

Yet the question remains whether these forms and methods of manipulation, brainwashing and conditioning can be used by dictatorships, thuggish regimes and rogue-states more successfully than by democracies with all their marketing techniques and paraphernalia. *Wag the Dog*, like other similar cinematographic productions, rests on the assumption of infinite manipulations as an offshoot or a side-effect of mass democracy. In so doing, it missed the point that military regimes can have much more success in this than their democratic adversaries. In fact, it is high time for the West to wake up and see the world around us for what it is. We are witnessing the resurgence of real – rather than velvet or imagined – totalitarianism in Russia. Public opinion was made and remade there as many times as the regime wanted it to be, and hatred for Ukraine was manufactured in accordance with the need for an enemy. Russia's talk of Ukraine's 'fascists' appropriates a term that best describes its user, for the more Russian propaganda speaks about Ukrainian fascism, the more of a family resemblance Russia itself bears to Nazi Germany, with all its hatred as a way of approaching reality, Goebbels-style propaganda and toxic lies.

Never before has George Orwell's *1984* and its vocabulary been as relevant as they are now, due to the sliding of Russia into barbarity and fascism with incredible speed and intensity. A series of interrogation scenes between O'Brien and Winston Smith, which alludes to the communists and the Nazis as the naïve predecessors of Oceania, who had an ideology, yet allowed their victims to become martyrs, sound now as the best wake-up call since Putinism entered its phase of war and terror: Newspeak, Two Minutes Hate, and the jackboot trampling on the human face for the sake of unlimited power have finally acquired the points of reference.

It is a fascism with no real ideology, for the set of tools used to boost the morale of its thugs and terrorists consists of worn-out clichés and recycled slogans largely borrowed from the Italian and Hungarian fascisms, with some Serbian additions from the times of Slobodan Milošević, and with Nazi cherries on top. Irredentism, the need to reunite the disunited nation, the world turned against the righteous people, the necessity to defend history for the sake of its re-enactment – these are all ghosts and spectres of twentieth-century fascism.

The tragedy of Russia is that its population is falling prey to the Kremlin's spin doctors with their ability to create virtual and TV hyper-reality that has hidden reality from the masses. Ukraine, for the Russian reincarnations and successors of Goebbels such as Vladislav Surkov, has become exactly what Albania was for Barry Levinson and his film – a piece of virtual reality fabricated for the sake of domestic policies. The funny thing is that the excessive and obsessive use of the term 'fascism' appears to be a form of cognitive dissonance in Russian fascism: be quick to apply your own name or title to portray your enemy – then you will appropriate the label and absolve yourself of it.

The winter of our discontent? As we know, *The Winter of Our Discontent* is the title of John Steinbeck's last novel, published in 1961. The title is a reference to the first two lines of William Shakespeare's *Richard III*: 'Now is the winter of our discontent / Made glorious summer by this sun of York.' Do we have the winter of our discontent now?

Zygmunt Bauman You suggest that Putin's Russia does not have an ideology. In fact, it is quite Orwellesque – 'the jackboot trampling on the human face', and power exercised for its own sake, as you put it. Your reference to Orwell feels flawless. By coincidence, Alena Ledeneva of University College London expanded on the grounds for that association in her post yesterday:

> One legacy shared by most survivors of oppressive political regimes is what George Orwell called 'doublethink' – which Yury Levada and Alexander Zinoviev branded as being the key feature of *Homo sovieticus*. Under late socialism, when present-day elites in Russia and Ukraine were growing up, it was irrelevant whether people believed official ideological messages or not. Instead, the relation to officialdom became based on intricate strategies of simulated support and on 'nonofficial' practices.

She also notes, however, that 'irreconcilable visions' of Russia held by the West and those made official in Russia, but increasingly also the popular, 'folkloristic' view, 'constitute a thesis and antithesis that co-exist without a possibility of synthesis, yet without an uncertainty as to what they are. The catch is that the clarity of polarized positions does not help in dealing with the complexities at hand.' Such a situation does not help us to find a 'working solution' to the present Russian–Ukrainian confrontation, nor does it help 'the West' to help Russia and Ukraine to find and apply one. To be of help, 'the West' – and particularly the US ('The United States' approach toward Russia [...] reflects traditional concerns, even phobias, based on an inadequate understanding of the country, in part because Russia has ceased to be a focus of U.S. foreign policy. The US approach to Ukraine is probably even less informed', opines Ledeneva) – needs to be aware of a considerably greater complexity to the situation than can be grasped or presented by the crude brushstrokes with which the mutually irreconcilable images are currently painted. For instance:

> The ambivalence of the Ukrainian elite can be defined as *substantive ambivalence*: they are Russian speaking, Russian educated, and Russian thinking individuals, who are fighting their own background; as *functional ambivalence*: they are criticising and

attacking a system that they themselves had been an integral part of; and as *normative ambivalence*: they are committing to pro-democratic values that contradict their political behaviour (for example, their position on the EU membership runs contrary to their business interests).[1]

Having added to this observation quite a few others equally acute and thought-inspiring, Ledeneva still feels the need to qualify her conclusions, confessing that 'The situation in Ukraine might be grasped best by a specialist on geopolitics, a scholar of the (il) legitimacy of power, an ethnographer of insurgencies, an analyst of media propaganda wars, a trauma therapist, or by a psychologist of phobias and love–hate relationships. I have none of these specialisms' – a confession that could be also mine in the same measure. Let me therefore leave the task of untying the Russian–Ukrainian version of the Gordian knot to those to whom it belongs by right – to all those specialisms, which I, just like Ledeneva, admit are absent from my toolbox, while being unable to acquire them at short notice. And let me move straight away to the area in which I feel a bit more confident: to the crucially important issue which you've raised – the problem of the capability of 'manipulation by political advertisement' to create in contemporary society 'people's needs and their criteria for happiness, but also [...] of fabricating the heroes of our time and controlling the imagination of the masses through laudatory biographies and success stories'. And in particular to the second of your queries, which, if answered in the affirmative, would qualify the message of the first: 'whether these forms and methods of manipulations, brainwashing and conditioning can be used by dictatorships, thuggish regimes and rogue-states more successfully than by democracies'.

But I don't think that the choice is between an affirmative and a negative answer – as the very nature of the manipulation, not just its effectiveness and chances of success, differs starkly between the two systems: dictatorship and democracy. In the final account, the difference boils down to that between 'hard' and 'soft' power. In democracies, the 'hard power' (the power of compulsion and enforcement, resting on the reduction of available options and raising the odds against undesirable options, as well as on application of force and its threat) has been reserved for those in the margins, who are unlikely to be responsive to temptations – that trademark of the 'soft power' strategy of domination. In dictatorships, application of force remains the principal ingredient of that strategy. When applied to the updated version of *1984*, that difference manifests itself in the tyrants', dictators' and auto-crats' preponderance for the monopoly of state-owned, state-monitored and state-managed channels of information, for silencing dissident views and persecution of their holders – all in all, for raising the personal costs of dissidence to a level that inspires/encourages/enforces subjects to internalize the practice of self-censorship and doublespeak (one language for private, another for public, settings and occasions). In democracies, however, with their preference for, and the prevalence of the significantly less costly 'soft power' variety of domination – power of temptation and seduction – for most subjects the means of an open-face casual coercion (which excludes 'economic coercion' from citizens' cal-culations, as a non-negotiable, constant, 'fact of life') remains at a distant horizon, as a problem of 'law and order' – and aimed therefore at 'them', not 'us', a coercion necessary to incapacitate 'their' trouble-making potential and force them away from causing trouble, while underpinning 'our' freedom and rights. With massive help from the media and consumer markets, democracy manages to convert social disaffection (now individual, personalized and privatized) from a liability into an asset; from a disruptive, anti-systemic force into a resource – a barrelful of grease lubricating its flywheels. I feel tempted to opine that democracy – not acci-dentally associated with the capitalist economy and consumerist culture – has fulfilled what all order-builders of all times dreamed of achieving but seldom did: for us to *wish* to do what we *must* do. Democracy in its present-day practice is more Huxleyan than Orwellian. Or rather it achieves Orwellian effects by deploying Huxleyan means, thus disposing of the need for a Ministry of Truth or Love.

To cut a long story short: I find it difficult to judge which socio-political system manipulates the minds and conduct of its subjects with more success. Neither one nor the other can do without manipulation. After all, the essence of order – any order, order as such – is, and cannot but be, manipulation of probabilities; in the case of social orders, of the probabilities of human behav-ioural choices. On top of its inhuman cruelty, manipulation dictatorial-style generates conflicts that it is incapable of either resolving or accommodating, and which for that reason lead in the longer run to its collapse. Also, it can neither absorb nor disarm the indissoluble and indestructible voluntarism of human subjects. On this score, democracy seems to be following English folk counsel: if you can't beat them, join them. Instead of bleeding itself to death, totalitarian-style, in a vain and fruitless war waged against the inalienable human freedom to choose, it has managed to deploy that freedom as one of its most efficient and altogether advantageous resources – verily, a feat inaccessible, and therefore incredible-sounding, to tyrants and dictators.

Professor Anna Wolff-Powęska has recently pointed out that the popular mood of the beginning of the twenty-first century is eerily reminiscent of the one dominant in Europe 100 years earlier, which then led to the world war and the birth of the two most formidable and grisly totalitarian regimes in history.[2] The constitutive traits of that mood are now, as they were then, 'a deep asymmetry between development of mostly scientific-technological civilization and the deficit, throughout Europe, of social sensitivity as well as a miserable moral condition of humans ready to deploy at any moment their destructive passions' and 'the feelings of being lost, uprooted with no one to trust', a mind-set eminently amenable to propagandist and populistic misuses. It was against such a background that many of the leading lights of the intellectual elite voiced their eulogies of the cleansing/purifying capacity of naked and brutal power, and it was thanks to that background that the eulogies were heard and avidly, joyfully listened to. Max Scheler wrote that 'iron and blood fertilize spirits', while Thomas Mann opined that war has the power to purify, liberate and offer hope that is otherwise absent or dashed. Having referred to a long list of the most distinguished and influential authors of the era, 'from Nietzsche and Sorel to Pareto, from Rimbaud and T. E. Lawrence to Jünger, Brecht and Malraux, from Bakunin and Nechayev to Aleksander Blok', Hannah Arendt concluded that so many authors were 'completely absorbed by their desire to see the ruin of this whole world of false security, fake culture, and fake life' and that 'Destruction without mitigation, chaos and ruins such assumed the dignity of supreme values.'[3] To growing numbers of the post-war generation, it seemed revolutionary 'to admit cruelty, disregard of human values, and general amorality, because this at least destroyed the duplicity upon which the existing society seemed to rest'.[4]

One century later, the expression 'May the Force be with you' has achieved an uncommonly massive cult status – confirmed by Wikipedia in a separate entry dedicated to its lightning-speed yet durable, spectacular career, started by the *Star Wars* movie series. Force as such, force for force's sake, force being by its nature a universal solution to all trouble and universal key to all doors – never in the whole series tied to a specific human task and specific purpose other than winning and defeating and thereby outliving 'the others'. *Star Wars* were among the most box-office successful films of all times; the cult that emerged then around the successive films in the series is thus far anything but exhausted, while the magic spell 'May the Force be with you' remains the most often-pronounced sentence in any encounter of their admirers and devotees.

Let's be wary of the temptation to console ourselves with laying the charge at the doorsteps of 'bad guys' like the Nazi or Stalinist 'hoodlums', while by the same token exonerating ourselves, the 'good guys', of any suspicion of complicity, and above all of the suspicion that, given the right conditions (such as permission from on high supported by a promise of impunity) for doing what they did, we might not be firm enough to refuse to do it on the strength of the values we cherish, the civilization we have been formed by, and the superior morality endemic to 'us' while absent in 'them'. 'National Socialism – or, more broadly, fascism', let me repeat, after Sontag, 'also stands for an ideal, and one that is also persistent today'. Certain inclinations may be chased underground, discredited and shamed, but they resist and emerge, by and large unscathed, from the civilizing drill, which – as Norbert Elias made us aware – surfs, rather than fathoms, our selves' morbid potential, when prohibiting us from spitting on the floor or – when sitting at a dinner table – putting meat (with its animal origin skilfully disguised by the lesser humans in the kitchen) in our mouths with a knife instead of a fork; or which – as Ervin Goffman found out – covers up (for better protection?) uncivil impulses with 'civil inattention'.

I am sad and sorry to feel obliged to admit having such apprehensions. I have recently been prompted even more to hold on to them by Grigory Shavlovich Chkhartishvili, writing under the penname of Boris Akunin – more precisely, by his *Aristonomia* ('Aristonomy') – an ambitious, wide-vistas and deep-breath novel encapsulating the history of Russia in the years immediately preceding and immediately following the Russian October Revolution, but a novel interspersed (literally) with still more ambitious philosophical essays, trying to crack the mystery of people he dubs 'aristonomes' (taking a leaf from the idea of aristocracy, as a class of noblemen epitomizing the virtue of nobility – but deciding to repossess and return that badge stolen by a privileged caste in order to defend their unearned and undeserved privileges while practising the opposite to what the stolen name would imply to its rightful owners, who really earned it by their deeds, not their hereditary titles). Apart from the reference to *aristos* ('excellent' in ancient Greek), the appellation 'aristonome' refers as well to *nomos* ('law'): for an aristonome, to excel is a law s/he wouldn't be able to ignore or transgress. S/he just can't do it, come what may – that inability being precisely the cause of his/her excellence. 'Ich kann nicht anders', was how Martin Luther explained his resolve to make public his condemnation of the corrupted, wallowing-in-lucre Roman Church, and to ignore the anathema that could follow his decision. And this is how the respondents to Nechama Tec, the author of the eye-opening study *When the Light Pierced the Darkness* – people who, despite the threat of the gallows, rushed to hide their Jewish neighbours earmarked for murder – answered her questions about their motives. And this is what those 10–15 per cent of people on the left slope of the Gauss curve (one recording the number of refusals to follow commands viewed as immoral) would probably answer, were they asked by Stanley Milgram, Philip Zimbardo, Christopher Browning or other researchers into human readiness to commit or refuse to commit an atrocity. Aristonomes recognize no judge more supreme than their conscience – as if they followed Albert Camus's principle: 'I rebel, therefore we exist.'

Akunin believes and tries to show that aristonomes are born and bred and matured in all classes – though in each class they constitute but a small, perhaps even minute, minority. And he adds, morosely that 'aristonomes' are ill equipped for the battle for survival – Darwin would have said they die like flies. Well, another apprehension which I am sad and sorry to confess is that on this point Akunin might be right.

Aristonomes, a small species living their lives under the cloud of impending extinction, are the people from whose ranks dissidents are recruited (more correctly, self-recruited). You ask: 'Do we have the winter of our discontent now?' You may gather from what has been said above that I am inclined to doubt it. This is so for many reasons, which we may yet have an opportunity to explore, but mainly because of what you probably had in mind when pointing out, again correctly, that Putin's Russia does not have an ideology. In that, though, Putin's Russia is not at all an exception. More likely, it may claim to represent a rule.

I already mentioned my comment published in *Eutopia* magazine on 8 November. I also quoted there, alongside you, Ivan Krastev – a most insightful observer of the meanders of our shared condition – from an article he published in the *Journal of Democracy* in October 2014. Allow me to quote him once more, this time in order to summon his help in answering your question:

> Some European countries stand today as classic examples of a crisis of democracy brought on by overly low stakes. Why should the Greeks or the Portuguese turn out to vote when they know perfectly well that, in the wake of the troubles associated with the euro, the policies of the next government will be just the same as those of the current one? In the days of the Cold War, citizens could resort to the urns with the expectation that their votes would decide their country's fate – whether it would stay part of the West or join the East, or whether private industry would be nationalized. Large, imposing questions were the order of the day. Today, the differences between left and right have essentially evaporated, and voting has become more about one's tastes than about anything that deserves the name of ideological conviction.
>
> Elections not only are losing their capacity to capture the popular imagination, they are failing to effectively overcome crises. People have begun to lose interest in them. There is a widespread suspicion that they have become a fool's game.[5]

I supplied that quotation with a supposition: that what most of us most of the time are fooled by, is our old acquaintance TINA ('There Is No Alternative', the creed of which Margaret Thatcher was the prime apostle and the first in the long line of bishops in the first of the great and rising number of its dioceses).

LD In his book of correspondence with Michel Houellebecq, *Public Enemies*, Bernard-Henri Lévy wrote on present-day Russia:

> Not only does this Russia inspire no desire in me, it fills me with horror. I'd go so far as to say that it frightens me because I see in it a possible destiny for the late-capitalist societies. Once upon a time, during your post-war 'glory days', the middle class was terrorized by being told that Brezhnev's communism was not an archaism restricted to distant societies but rather a picture of our own future. We were wrong: it was not communism but postcommunism, Putinism, that may be the testing ground for our future.[6]

How true! That Putinism is far from the madman's follies whose mention would suffice to prove the political and moral superiority of European values is obvious to anyone not devoid of a sense of reality. Lion Feuchtwanger, André Gide or Jean-Paul Sartre – that is, European writers and thinkers infatuated with the Soviet Union as a rival civilization to the West (as Ernest Gellner once put it so aptly) – are all old news. And the real and hot news about the Kremlin's new apprentices in Europe is less about Gerhard Schroeder and what Edward Lucas termed the Schroederization of the European political classes, than about this new disturbing phenomenon.

The former Soviet Union was a Shakespearean tragedy. The Second World War and the defeat of the Nazis, unthinkable without the heroism and sacrifices of Russians, Ukrainians and other nations of the former USSR, provided the Kremlin with a historical-political narrative which partly softened the horrors of Bolshevism and Stalinism. After all, wasn't it the USSR that dealt a mortal blow to the Nazis and that shouldered the greatest burden of the Second World War? After Stalin's death, a certain *modus vivendi* was worked out between the West and the USSR, and equating Nazism or fascism with the USSR, no matter how tempting it was after the Holodomor and all the other horrors of Stalinism, was the last thing that European or American academics and journalists would have done.

The USSR won much sympathy and support from Europe's and America's Left in terms of their shared critical attitude to the iniquities in their societies, not to mention such core sensitivities of the Left as the working-class people and their exploitation, down-and-outs in big industrial cities, etc. Today's Russia with its image in the West as a country of tycoons with luxurious mansions in France and Spain, as well as its billionaires so admired in the City of London as cash cows, would have appeared in the old days of the USSR as the worst kind of nightmare, if not as a series of political cartoons in a Soviet magazine published with the aim of poking fun at the bourgeoisie in the West.

In addition, great Russian poets, actors, film and theatre directors have greatly contributed to the sense of the tragedy of Eastern Europe: while the USSR has richly deserved the immortal writings of Nikolai Gogol or Nikolai Leskov or Mikhail Saltykov-Shchedrin for its grotesque political life that was publicly depicted as genuine democracy and freedom, the geniuses of twentieth-century Russian culture – such as composers Sergei Prokofiev and Dmitry Shostakovich, writers and poets Mikhail Bulgakov, Osip Mandelstam and Boris Pasternak, writers and translators Ilya Ehrenburg and Samuil Marshak, or film directors Grigory Kozintsev and Andrei Tarkovsky – have become the best counterpoint to the portrayal of Soviet Russia as a country of barbarians. It was a continuous tragedy for the nation whose politics was sinister, devilish, and posed an existential threat to the entire world, yet whose magnificent culture was the best redeemer from the moral and political disaster created by the aforementioned state. Modern Russian culture appears to have been the best antidote against the tyrannical state of Russia and its political barbarity.

The Latvian film director Dāvis Sīmanis's half-documentary film *Escaping Riga* (2014) offers a point of departure for dealing with the intrinsic logic of evil in the twentieth century. Modelled after what we may well call the 'mockumentary' (in terms of cinematographic language, it bears a family resemblance to Woody Allen's masterpiece *Zelig*), this film deals with two people of genius. Both were born in Riga, Latvia. Both had turbulent lives, though they lived at the same time in two drastically different political settings, and even in two opposing and irreconcilable civilizations. Both had their Jewish connection enriched by a Baltic flavour. Both risked their lives participating in the dramas of the twentieth century. Both achieved fame. The two people in question masterfully portrayed in Sīmanis's film are the British political theorist and historian of ideas Sir Isaiah Berlin, and the Soviet film director Sergei Eisenstein.

Isaiah Berlin (1909–97), a perfect speaker of Russian, was from his youngest days interested not only in Russian culture but in the ideas and history of the Baltic region as well. Having later become a world-famous political theorist and historian of ideas, he continued his preoccupation with that region's greatest thinkers: Immanuel Kant, Johann Gottfried von Herder, and especially the man who inspired the latter, Johann Georg Hamann. Hamann was born and lived in Königsberg, died in Münster, and was held to be a genius by his contemporaries who called him the 'Magus of the North'. Berlin's interest in Hamann (whose friendship with Kant did not prevent him from being one of his great opponents and who considered emotions to be more important than reason) most likely was behind his theoretical attention to a phenomenon he called the Counter-Enlightenment.

The reach of Isaiah Berlin's works is immense. They include books about great epochs of European thought and culture, the Renaissance and the Romantic age; about Russian thinkers and writers; about Niccolò Machiavelli; about conceptions of freedom, liberalism and nationalism; about European conflicts and the quest for peace. He was a thinker and political actor, all in one. To be an active diplomat and public figure and then to immerse himself in the life of Oxford University and create new institutions and research programmes there was as natural to him as moving from one subject matter to another. There are quite a few studies about Isaiah Berlin's connections to the greats of Russian culture – from Anna Akhmatova to Andrei Sakharov.

The Baltic region is usually associated with late Romantic and neo-Romantic movements, and conservative nationalism in particular. That's a cliché. Recalling the great liberal thinkers from that region – Immanuel Kant, Johann Gottfried von Herder, Paul Schiemann and Isaiah Berlin – is all it takes to reveal the fact that the Baltic lands gave the world many more prominent representatives of modern liberalism than other similarly sized European countries have. By the same token Isaiah Berlin and Paul Schiemann join the ranks of those twentieth-century thinkers who remained non-indoctrinated, antitotalitarian and did not succumb to hatred, a list that includes Hannah Arendt, Karl R. Popper, Leszek Kołakowski, Czesław Miłosz, Alexander Shtromas and Tomas Venclova. As we can see, most of them have ties to the Baltics.

Things were different with Sergei Eisenstein (1898–1948). Born
into the family of a German-Jewish father and Russian Orthodox
mother, Sergei departed from his family's initial trajectories of
faith. A Russian Orthodox believer in his childhood, Sergei became
an ardent atheist; unlike his father who was a staunch supporter
of the Whites, he was to become a brother-in-arms to the Reds.
A great cinematic innovator, Eisenstein is widely and justly
regarded as the father of the montage technique pivotal in the art
of the cinema.

He was not entirely different from his great British counterpart,
though. Like Isaiah Berlin, Sergei Eisenstein remained a mystery
both for his fellow countrymen and countrywomen and for his
hosts elsewhere. Admired for his talent, innovativeness and bold-
ness by such celebrities as Charlie Chaplin, Theodore Dreiser and
Upton Sinclair in the USA, and later by Frida Kahlo and Diego
Rivera in Mexico, Eisenstein began describing his films as 'moving
frescoes', anticipating the greatest film directors of the twentieth
century, such as Pier Paolo Pasolini, Federico Fellini, Michelangelo
Antonioni and Andrei Tarkovsky, all of whom were legitimate
heirs to the legacy of Renaissance and Baroque art.

Eisenstein was forced to interrupt his enchanting life of travel
and experiment abroad after Joseph Stalin made it clear that he
had to return to the USSR. Long suspected of having abandoned
the aesthetics of socialist realism, Eisenstein survived the Stalinist
purges in a rather miraculous way. There is little doubt that it was
only through the great success of his patriotic – not to say nation-
alistic – film *Aleksandr Nevsky* (1938), and Stalin's favourite film,
Ivan the Terrible, in particular (two parts, 1944–5), that Eisenstein
was left in peace, and even received the Order of Lenin and the
Stalin Prize. The same applies to a bunch of other fortunate geniuses, such as Mikhail Bulgakov, Sergei Prokofiev, Boris Pasternak
and Dmitry Shostakovich, who miraculously survived in the
Devil's State.

Did Eisenstein and Berlin meet? Yes, they did. It happened once
in Moscow after the Second World War. Through Dāvis Sīmanis's
film *Escaping Riga*, we are given a broad perspective on the twentieth century with all its paradoxes and disturbing complexities.

In my book on politics and literature, which has been translated
into Ukrainian, I made honourable mention of Mikhail Bulgakov

and his work of genius, *The Master and Margarita* (1966–7). The Ukrainian-born writer, whose dissenting voice in Russian literature was silenced for decades, anticipated the emergence of modern barbarity. His masterpieces, such as the novel just mentioned (which is a modern – and essentially East European – version of the tale of Faust, but this time one about a woman who gives her soul to the Devil in exchange for her beloved man, a cornered and anguished writer confined to a mental asylum), allow us to regard this great Ukrainian and Russian writer as having been for Eastern Europe what Kafka was for Central Europe. He was a prophet of the modern forms of evil, or of the Devil in politics, if you prefer.

In addition to being politically and morally incisive, as we see in his novels and stories, such as *The Heart of a Dog* or *The Fatal Eggs* – both inter-textual, each anticipating the other and also paving the way for *The Master and Margarita* – Bulgakov is the brightest example of what theorists call *the anxiety of physical destruction*, as opposed to *the anxiety of influence*: the anxiety of influence appears to be more widespread in the West, whereas the anxiety of physical destruction seems more characteristic of Eastern Europe.

The sense of the surreal, grotesque and absurd is widely believed – and with sound reason – to have been deeply grounded in Eastern and Central European literature. In fact, it reached Parisian literary circles through Eugène Ionesco, yet it was also manifest in such Polish writers as Witold Gombrowicz and Stanisław Ignacy Witkiewicz. If we can derive this form of literary sensitivity and of the representation of the world from Jonathan Swift, then we should add immediately that the genius of Ukrainian literature, Nikolai Gogol, was very much an East European Swift. A major figure in Eastern European literature, Gogol may have been the father of the modern political fable based on a strong sense of the absurd. No matter how uniquely distinct and incomparable these writers are in terms of style and form, they best caught and expressed what was the Zeitgeist of their age.

It was with good reason that Arthur Koestler once called his close friend George Orwell a missing link between Jonathan Swift and Franz Kafka. Without a shadow of a doubt, we could confer similar roles in Eastern European and world literature on the geniuses of Ukraine's multilingual, rich, and magnificent literature, such as Nikolai Gogol, Mikhail Bulgakov, Sholem Aleichem,

Sigizmund Krzhizhanovsky, Isaac Babel, Ilya Ilf, Yevgeny Petrov and Yuri Olesha, to name just a few.

Or we could recall Paul Celan, a great Ukrainian-born Romanian-Austrian poet whose name was engraved in golden letters on the German-speaking world's literary map as a reference to the best in post-war European poetry. A poet of genius, and a translator of Russian poetry, including Osip Mandelstam, Paul Celan immortalized his name with *Todesfuge* (1948; 'Death Fugue') – one of the greatest-ever poems on the Shoah. Thus, Ukraine is quite a fertile soil for thought, moral imagination and sensitivity that covers an immense territory of modern experience, from the comic to the tragic.

Playing a subtle game with literary allusions, Timothy Snyder once stressed Gogol's *Nose* as a symbol of the absurdity and deformity of Russia's tyrannical state and the seemingly powerful, albeit grotesque, bureaucracy it produced. Yet the former President of Ukraine, Viktor Yanukovych, appears in Snyder's essay as a character losing his hands, instead of his nose – hands that have a life story of their own. These are hands that can steal or beat up an innocent person.[7] We badly need a Gogol for our time who would point out what else has been lost by Eastern European politics. This would shed more light on Western Europe's deformities as well.

Elsewhere, Timothy Snyder has pointed out that, if we want to understand Putin, we have to read Orwell.[8] First and foremost, he was referring to the phenomenon of Doublethink, which allowed the people of Oceania to hold two mutually contradictory and even exclusive truths at one and the same time. In this situation, you become skilled at being oppressed to such a degree that you find yourself capable of switching from one truth to another, once you notice that the time of the first has passed and the time for the second has come. If you manage to reconcile in your head the balance of two mutually irreconcilable facts – that there are no Russian troops in Crimea (as nobody has yet identified the insignia and background of the little green men), and that there is some limited military presence in Crimea to relieve the pain of the local population – then you can congratulate yourself on successfully passing the exam.

The same applies perfectly to the Donbass region: there is no Russian military there, just some rebels – yet you have to negotiate with Russia over the region whose status is to be determined by more than Ukraine and its legislation. We are here, and we are not here, at one and the same time – a puzzle of politics which can be solved only by those who still possess the gift of undeniable political intuition regarding how to reveal the whim and indulgence of those in power. The ability to sustain and keep Doublethink in action appears as sort of postmodern game whose players poke fun at what we take for postmodernist epistemology and what Friedrich Nietzsche would have described as nihilism: nothing exists, nothing is there, it is just a trick of your imagination – yet something may well be there if you change your perspective and social viewpoint.

In 2015, we marked sixty-five years since George Orwell's death. He appears to have been the real prophet of totalitarianism, and far and away the most insightful writer in the West, who got the very essence of the tragedy of Eastern Europe. With sound reason, then, the Russian poet, translator and dissident Natalya Gorbanevskaya called George Orwell an honorary citizen of Eastern Europe.

A Left-winger who was bound to exemplify his political views in his own life, Orwell was a maverick and dissenter among those who were inclined to think about themselves as mavericks and dissenters by vocation. Fiercely attacked by his fellow Leftists in Great Britain as a traitor – or, at best, as a fellow traveller – Orwell avoided the ideological blindness and selective sensitivity so widespread among his brothers-in-arms. Like Ignazio Silone described by Czesław Miłosz as one of the most decent political figures in Europe, Orwell held humanity to be prior and superior to the doctrine, and not the other way around.

A passionate collision took place between Orwell and the Left in Great Britain over whether valuing one's roots was a supposedly bourgeois and reactionary concept. Deracination was always favoured by the Left as a sign of personal liberty and dignity, yet Orwell tried to reconcile natural patriotic feelings with other modern sensibilities – first and foremost with individual freedom, dignity, equality and fellowship. He believed that our existential need for roots and a home, if neglected – or, worse, despised – could make an awkward comeback in the form of symbolic compensation, such as a fierce attachment to the doctrine or ideology that becomes our symbolic home. Our homelessness calls for compensation, which comes in the form of ideological substitutes. As Karl Marx would have had it himself, a genuine proletarian does not have a home, for his home is socialism.

In his essay 'Notes on Nationalism' (1945), Orwell drew a strict dividing line between patriotism, which he understood as identification with a way of life and all earthly forms of human attachment, and nationalism, which appeared to him to be a belief that one's group is superior to and better than other groups. What results from such a divide, according to Orwell, is a carefully disguised propensity to classify human individuals as if they were communities of bees or ants. Whereas patriotism is silent and defensive, nationalism is offensive and aggressive.

Apart from several major radical forms of nationalism, and ideological zeal and fervour in general, nationalism can come in many guises. According to Orwell, the transferred or transposed forms of nationalism signify our desire to find an object of worship, which may vary from time to time. A pious Zionist may become an ardent Marxist, or the other way around, while it takes little effort to move from Left-wing views to uncritical adoration of Russia, even failing to notice Russian imperialism and colonialism.

G. K. Chesterton's love for Italy and France led him as far as failing to notice the emergence of Mussolini and Italian fascism, whereas H. G. Wells was blinded by Russia to such an extent that he refused to see the crimes of Lenin and Stalin. That our propensity to fool and deceive ourselves is nearly limitless was closely and wittily observed by the perceptive British journalist and writer who easily surpassed all British and European thinkers put together in his ability to foresee the tragedy of Europe. Orwell's critical essays appear to have been even more original and groundbreaking than his famous satires and dystopias.

Orwell's *Animal Farm* has been widely and justly celebrated worldwide, and yet little attention was paid to the fact that it was the Ukrainian writer Nikolai Kostomarov (1817–85) who preceded and anticipated Orwell's vision, becoming the first writer to depict the future Russian revolution in the form of an allegory about the rebellion of animals against their masters. We will never know whether Orwell knew of Kostomarov's fable, but we do know that he was perfectly well aware of the Holodomor as well as the tragedy of Ukraine, since he wrote the 'Preface for the Ukrainian Reader' in the Ukrainian edition of his celebrated social and political satire.

His masterpiece *1984* was not altogether original either. Orwell really owed much to Yevgeny Zamyatin, whose novel *We* (1923) served as a great source of inspiration not only for his *1984* but for Aldous Huxley's *Brave New World* as well. Yet, whereas there is not a single mention of or word of credit to Zamyatin in Huxley's work, Orwell acknowledged the genius of Zamyatin in the review he wrote for the British edition of *We* (incidentally, it saw the light of day after a good deal of delay, compared with the American edition which came out much earlier). The point was that Orwell received from Pyotr Struve the manuscript of Zamyatin's *We* in French. At that time, Struve, having escaped from the Bolshevik terror, lived in Paris. The author of *Down and Out in Paris and London* spoke French, and it took little if any effort to appreciate fully the superb literary quality of *We*. In all likelihood, *1984* has become a variation on all the major themes developed in *We*, with an added stroke of genius.

However, influenced by Zamyatin, George Orwell, much to his credit, was quite profound in showing the nuances of thought, such as Winston Smith's petty attachment to his favourite little things – a seemingly bourgeois weakness for which Orwell was severely criticized by Raymond Williams and other critics. His keen predictions have become history – for example, his sombre vision of the death of privacy, the colonization of human sexuality, and infinite control over us through the tyranny of the TV screen. For this, Orwell will long be remembered as a true prophet of our present condition.

George Orwell, among other things, predicted and anticipated Putinism as an ideology-free form of political gangsterism and fascism better than anybody else.

The transition from the Kafkaesque to the Orwellesque marks the dividing line between solid and liquid evil, as you would have it, Zygmunt: in Kafka's world before the Second World War, we would have failed to understand why and how all this should have happened to us – it just happened, leaving no trace of clarity and logic in the air, yet we would know that there was an alternative which was to be seen sooner or later; in Orwell's world, we do

understand why and how, yet there is little or even nothing we
can do about it, as there is no alternative at all. Do it yourself –
this is the logic of liquid evil. And you do. They make you do it
by yourself. You – and not them – yell 'Don't do it to me, do it
to Julia.' In the end, you love Big Brother.

Everything is denied or reinvented. Everything is made and
unmade on a daily basis. Those who control the past control the
future. Those who control the present control the past. Those who
control TV control reality. Those who control the Internet control
imagination and the principle of an alternative. Those who control
the media control the territories. Those who control TV channel
anguish into hatred, manufacturing love for Big Brother and
hatred for Emmanuel Goldstein. Needless to say, the Two Minutes
Hate is straight from Oceania. Collective hysteria, as well as its
translation into political action or legitimation of policies, becomes
a means to legitimacy and truth – or rather what Erich Fromm
defined as mobile truth, which is transferable to any situation,
conflict or war.

Yet there is one more aspect of the Orwellesque which shaped
our present political landscape significantly. 'War is peace', claims
the Party in Oceania. As soon as the situation changes on the
ground, switching the interchangeable alliances and animosities
from Eurasia (another spark of genius which led Orwell as far as
Putin's political fantasies about a rival civilization and political
union able to outweigh the EU) to Eastasia (the third fictional
superstate in *1984*, a rival and an ally to Oceania and Eurasia at
one and the same time), the logic may change completely. 'Peace
is war', claims the Party conversely, and, again, those who contrive
to switch to this revelation immediately are on the winning side.
They wouldn't expose their weakness and inability to get all the
big things right – only those who fail to do so would be downed.
'You don't exist', O'Brien tells Winston Smith, as if to say that it
is the Party that grants existence to individuals, rather than any
other form of ever-presence.

What remains behind the world of the political action and
mental acrobatics of the elite, combined with the fanaticism of the
masses – whether sincere and long-term or situational and short-
term – is the fact that low-intensity conflicts can change the logic
of war and peace considerably. Territory is not an issue nowadays,
and all territorial claims are merely a tactical manoeuvre to hide
the real objective, which lies in political destabilization, social

disempowerment and dismemberment of citizens, and, finally, disruption of life. Intimidation with the aim of planting fear and distrust in people's perception of reality is the real goal of Orwellesque politics. Like Winston Smith and Julia who are bound to lose their love and powers of association for the benefit of Oceania, the Inner Party and Big Brother, societies can lose their visions, alternatives, hopes and forms of faith. The world without alternatives can be employed by all forces that foster social determinism and political fatalism – from technocracy masquerading as democracy in the West, to overtly dictatorial, neo-imperialist, revisionist and revenge-seeking states such as Russia.

How prophetic was Orwell in his ground-breaking dystopia? Quite so, as we can see now. Emmanuel Goldstein's secret treatise, *Theory and Practice of Oligarchic Collectivism*, appears as the best clue to understanding oligarchy as a form of governance in Russia, supplemented with a fierce denial of political liberty, individual ethics, and most modern moral and political sensibilities, yet up-to-date in its approach to science and technology. To recall Jean Baudrillard's idea of a simulacrum,[9] the war-is-peace-and-peace-is-war mind-set and the message it keeps sending hide the fact that there is nothing left of either in this world: neither war nor peace exists any longer in their previous form. Instead, we see their constant interchangeability and their merging.

When and how did we lose our faith in humanity? Orwell suggested in his diaries more than once that one of the most horrible things to experience is the collapse of our ideals, including disenchantment with people we would normally credit as decent and kind.[10] Panic-mongering and defeatism are just the beginning of what may happen if the aggressor strikes your country, according to him.

For instance, Orwell could not help thinking about the awful possibility of collaborationism in Great Britain, should Germany have occupied it. He was convinced that the vast majority of the British establishment and elite would have unavoidably started collaborating with Hitler and the Nazis. The brutality of the Nazis, as well as their military superiority, he thought, would have forced British policemen, part of the military, and even the political class, to take sides with or apparently accept the Nazis and their domination.[11]

No matter how insightful Orwell was, he was proved wrong in not thinking highly of his fellow Brits, who heroically withstood the bombing of London and Coventry, and who were sufficiently strong to crush, along with the Allies, a major evil of the twentieth century. Orwell, an unconventional Left-winger and non-doctrinaire socialist, even contrived to be greeted and embraced by the Tories as a prodigal son whose alleged return to the Right was celebrated after the release of *1984* – due not only to the fact that the main character of his dystopia, Winston Smith, bore the first name of Churchill, but also to his merciless attacks on Ingsoc – that is, English socialism, described by Orwell as a gravedigger for personal freedom, political liberty and human dignity.

Whatever the case, his good fortune saved him from disdain for his country's elite as well as from the loss of faith in humanity in general. The Tory Winston Churchill became his hero as a result of the moral and political leadership Churchill gave to his nation when Britain needed it the most. Thus, the novel intended as *The Last European* was to become *1984*, with Winston Smith as its protagonist as if to immortalize the name of the one who had the guts and the willpower not to succumb to evil. Just like Mikhail Bulgakov who despised fear, George Orwell thought of fear as the most dehumanizing threat that could result in the collapse of society as an existential meeting point and hotbed of two main things in human life – the powers of individuality and the powers of association.

Zygmunt Bauman   You offer a breath-taking and blood-curdling survey of politics – 'from technocracy masquerading as democracy in the West, to overtly dictatorial, neo-imperialist, revisionist, and revenge-seeking states such as Russia'. The modalities differ, in many respects sharply, but in one crucial and most worrying respect – fostering 'social determinism and political fatalism' – they both score highly; there is not much to choose between them. Indeed, a spectre is haunting Europe: the spectre of the *absence of alternative* – particularly of a fully and truly attractive alternative, an alternative that promises to put paid to that ambiance of fatalism, impotence, collapse of imagination. This is a kind of crisis, with a dark tunnel at the end of the light; frustrated hopes married to lack of prospects. How far we have gone, in those twenty-five years separating us from the fall of the Berlin Wall and from the boisterous proclamations of the final and ultimate triumph of democracy? At one end of the spectrum, there are Putin-style post-Orwellian experiments with 'managed democracy'; at the other, a democracy more Huxleyan than Orwellian – or, rather, a democracy that achieves Orwellian effects by deploying Huxleyan means and – I repeat – has no need for Ministries of Truth or Love as their functions have been decentralized and subsidiarized to their individually administered DIY mini-replicas.

A tunnel at the end of the light (a phrase that Claus Offe coined, prophetically, in the aftermath of the fall of the Berlin Wall): quite a few of us would find that vision unjustified and misleading. Isn't the most remarkable mark of the current moment, on the contrary, that people are setting out earnestly in search of alternatives to the ways of doing politics that are ever more obviously indolent, incapable of and unwilling to recycle human preferences into social realities, and all in all bankrupt in their assumed task of promoting the human freedom of self-assertion? And they do so armed with unprecedentedly mighty and effective weapons supplied by the cutting-edge technology of communication – now lateral, instead of the vertical form in which bureaucratized politics excelled? Krastev, in the already quoted article, effectively debunks that kind of presumption:

As information and communication technologies spread, public life is becoming more democratized and individuals are becoming more empowered. People can know more with greater speed and organize themselves more quickly and easily than ever before, raising a threat to authoritarian regimes. At the same time, however, the rise of 'Big Data' in politics is allowing governments and large corporations to gather, organize, and instantly access nearly unlimited amounts of information about the preferences and behavior patterns of citizens. The possibilities for manipulation (sometimes traveling under the benign-sounding label of 'nudging') and even coercion are obvious, as is the threat thereby posed to the foundations of democracy. Both nudging elites and protesting masses have this in common: The new information technologies facilitate their activities, and neither group finds the people's preferences as expressed through the ballot box to be of more than minor importance. Elites approach elections as opportunities for manipulating the people rather than listening to them (Big Data makes voting marginal as a source of feedback), while protesters prefer to use elections as occasions for demonstrations rather than as tools to shape policy.

Alternatives with a sporting chance of replacing the extant, clearly outdated and inept ways of doing politics (and especially the present model of democracy) are precisely the things which the 'square people' (a phrase coined by Thomas Friedman), pitching tents for a few days – or a few weeks at the utmost – on Tahrir, Maidan Nezalezhnosti, Taksim, Bolotnaya, Rothschild, Puerta del Sol, Syntagma, Altamira or Zuccotti squares, parks or boulevards, are organically incapable of inventing – and even less of forcing the political bodies to embrace.

> None of the major protest movements has come out with a platform for changing the world – or even the economy. In this sense, we may be looking less at a possible engine of revolutionary activity against capitalism than at one of capitalism's safety valves [...] The protests everywhere succeeded in disrupting the political status quo, but they also helped the elites to relegitimize their power by, in effect, demonstrating that there is no real alternative to them [...] It is a moment, not a movement. It is an explosion of political subjectivity, and like any explosion, it by definition cannot be sustained.[12]

Protest 'movements' (I much prefer to call them, following Krastev's suggestion, 'protest *moments*') tell us quite a lot about what people don't want – though very little, if anything at all, about what they desire instead. We know they are furious with their alleged representatives' insensitivity to their plight, desires and postulates, as well as the rulers' evident incapacity (and presumed lack of will) to do anything to lift, or at least to mitigate, their misery. We surmise, sensibly, that what prompts them to gather in public squares is the need to unload their long-accumulated mistrust and anger, and to show just how strongly they are felt. We may as well conjecture that they are frightened by the direction in which things crucially important to them are moving, and determined to awake the powers-that-be from their coma and force them to change that direction – but we don't know where to. I suggest, though, that, to this question, Franz Kafka answered for the 'square people' long before they took to the streets in protest:

> I heard the sound of a trumpet, and I asked my servant what it meant. He knew nothing and had heard nothing. At the gate he

stopped me and asked: 'Where is the master going?' 'I don't know', I said, 'just out of here, just out of here. Out of here, nothing else, it's the only way I can reach my goal.' 'So you know your goal?' he asked. 'Yes', I replied. 'I've just told you. Out of here – that's my goal.'[13]

And a second answer, complementing the first:

No one, no one at all, can blaze a trail to India. Even in his day the gates to India were beyond reach, yet the King's sword pointed the way to them. Today the gates have receded to remoter and loftier places; no one points the way; many carry swords, but only to brandish them, and the eye that tries to follow them is confused.[14]

In their *Generatives of the World, Unite!* – a 'manifesto' prepared for publication in Amedeo D'Adamo's English translation – Mauro Magatti and Chiara Giaccardi give a valuable hint to all of us who try hard to crack that puzzle of no one being able to 'blaze a trail to India' any longer. They direct our attention to the unanticipated consequences of creating a society in which – having shed our chains, together with the traces they left in our memory and the stray and erratic fears of their return – 'we all want to be free, and if we are free then we want to be *more* free'. In such a society – our Western society, but not (yet?) its Eastern counterpart – we want

to keep open all possibilities, we force ourselves into the fleeting moment, naïvely delivered into the moment that you can never repeat. [...] Paradoxically, choice itself becomes constraint, in that it reduces possibilities: thus in the end we refrain from choosing. Or rather, only those choices become acceptable that do not bind the future and that, as such, are crushed in the instant.

Those words, I believe, convey the state of the political game in the West – though only its future (?) in the East. The West and the East of Europe, I am inclined to suggest, share astronomical time – but not historical time. Nelson Mandela, in his memoir *Long Walk to Freedom*, alerted us to the consequences of that anachronism:

When I walked out of prison, that was my mission, to liberate the oppressed and the oppressor both. Some say that has now been achieved. But I know that that is not the case. The truth is that we are not yet free; we have merely achieved the freedom to be free, the right not to be oppressed. We have not taken the final step of our journey, but the first step on a longer and even more difficult road. For to be free is not merely to cast off one's chains, but to live in a way that respects and enhances the freedom of others. The true test of our devotion to freedom is just beginning.

Whereas Magatti and Giaccardi unpack Mandela's message pointing out that to avoid

excessive and ever-present dangers, it should be recognized that 'freedom during freedom' presents separate issues from those of 'freedom under duress'. Advanced democracies have not yet addressed this cultural shift. This delay prevents us from recognizing that the most serious threats to freedom today derive not from a lack of freedom but from the essentially unexpected consequences of freedom released.

To cut the long story short: I wholeheartedly agree with your suggestion that pointing out what 'has been lost by Eastern European politics' 'would shed more light on Western Europe's deformities as well'; but I suspect that focusing on 'what has been lost' in Eastern European politics is somewhat misleading – as nothing that hasn't as yet been had can be 'lost'. The essential freedom of human individuals that is self-evident in Western Europe – after a centuries-long uphill struggle having become self-evident to the extent of being tacitly assumed and thus unreflected upon ('zuhanden', as Heidegger would say) – in Eastern Europe had neither sufficient time nor opportunity to assume the 'vorhanden' modality, – meaning to be noticed and noted with all its mysteries and paradoxes, perceived as simultaneously an object of not-yet-complete cognition and comprehension in urgent need of completion, and a clarion call to action. If we do what you suggest we could and ought to be doing, we will indeed 'shed more light' on Western Europe's deformities – but thanks to exposing and unravelling the *different* nature of the rather novel kind of 'deformities' that haunt the West, compared to those that haven't as yet been left behind in the East and are still vivid in the collective memory and in the habits drilled and the worldview instilled in the long era of un-freedom. In the West as much as in the East of Europe, democracy faces awesome dangers – but the menaces they confront come from different sources and manifest themselves in different sets of 'deformities'.

That said, sharing astronomical time in a world criss-crossed by information highways must be prolific in spawning hybrid amalgams patched from quite diverse influences and inspiration, and most likely to pollute the pristine purity of ideal types (a realization manifested in the popularity of the 'multiple modernities' concept). Dichotomy is useful as a heuristic device; it would be wrong, however, to treat is as an empirical juxtaposition of two complete, self-sufficient and self-contained totalities.

3

Where Are the Great Promises of Modernity to Be Found?

Fear and Loathing in the Brave New World

Leonidas Donskis At the beginning of the twenty-first century, we are likely to live in the world where the successful exercise of power, be it plausible violence or good economic performance, increasingly becomes a licence to abandon individual freedom, civil liberties and human rights. Alas, no social networking, mass education or emerging global sensibilities can alter this logic of things.

From the time of Niccolò Machiavelli onwards a quiet revolution has taken place in the world of human awareness and sensibility. If the criterion and definition of truth given by, among others, Thomas Aquinas (the correspondence of a thing to the intellect: *adaequatio rei et intellectus*) was still operative in science and philosophy, it undoubtedly ceased to hold in practical life and politics, where it was no longer believed that power derived from God and that politics was intrinsically an abode of virtue and a form of wisdom. The modern revolution engineered by Machiavelli's political thought is best embodied in his concept of *verità effettuale* ('efficacious truth'), whereby truth becomes practice – in fact, practical action. Truth in politics is produced by the person who generates action and achieves results, but not by the person who defines, articulates and questions, in the light of virtue, that action and those results, or examines them in the context of the classical canon. This is to say that truth is success, and, conversely, success is truth.

The politician who creates an enduring practice, who transforms an idea into an action, and who institutionalizes that idea is the one who has truth on his side. How he does all that is of secondary importance. It is not a goal that justifies means, but an actor who wedges his sceptics and critics, from all periods and from a variety of cultures, into the same form of politics and life that comes to be considered right, historical and immortal. Truth is whatever stays in the memory, while failure is condemned to die and to be stigmatized as a fiasco and a shame. Survival at the cost of virtue and higher morality sounds forth as an early rallying cry of the modern world; only later would that voice be distorted by Social Darwinists and racists into the symbolic centre of the struggle to survive.

The tyrant who has centralized the state and liquidated his opponents becomes father of his nation, while a despot who has tried to do the same but has lost out or has failed to reach all his goals earns universal scorn and is decisively forgotten. Forces that have successfully executed a *coup d'état* or revolution become heroic insurrectionists against reactionary, morally bankrupt institutions, but if they are unsuccessful they become mere conspirators or rioters. Shame and stigma attach not to a refusal of virtue, to an embrace of wickedness, and to an active choice of evil, but to a loss of power, to an inability to hold on to it, to suffering defeat. Power is honoured, but utter powerlessness or even just weakness does not deserve a philosophical conception of its own or any kind of sympathy. In this paradigm, sympathy and compassion are due only to those who do not participate in the sphere of power. But if you are in it, it is either success that awaits you, or else death and disappearance. Death can be a simple forgetting: they are the same.

That is why in this paradigm of modern instrumentalism, treachery is easily justified: if it ends in the retention or expansion of power, it is easy to position it as a painful sacrifice in the name of the state or as a big and common purpose or ideal. But if the treachery ends in failure and the conspirators cause a fiasco, then with help from symbolic authority and the state machinery it is securely placed in the exalted category of supreme disloyalty to the state – *high treason*. If the conspiracy went well and the head of state or of the institution is liquidated or at least compromised, then the conspirators become patriots and statesmen; but if the old system prevails and sweeps up all those who organized the conspiracy, the latter are not only destroyed but left to history as traitors and persons incapable of loyalty, i.e., as all-round weaklings.

Finally, there is also a metaphysics of treachery: it can be explained as disappointment with former friends, partners, companions-in-arms and ideals, but that doesn't change the heart of the matter. A treachery interpreting itself this way sounds like a naïve hostage to self-created disappointment and to the discovery of a new world, but its deep causes lie somewhere else. In our time, treachery has become the chance, fortune and practice of situational man, a pragmatist and instrumentalist torn from his human essence and isolated from and by other people. As is well known, remorse and guilt today have become political commodities in games of public communication, just like carefully dosed-out hatred. Perhaps infidelity has become not so much an article of trade as an element of instrumental reason and situational virtue.

In a world of intermittent human ties and of inflated words and vows, faithlessness no longer shocks. When fidelity ceases to be at the centre of our personality and a force that integrates all of a human being's identity, then treachery becomes a situational 'norm' and 'virtue'. What happens to politics then? It becomes a haven for people of situational – or, as Erich Fromm once called it, mobile – truth. It easily lends itself to adventure-seekers, criminals and crooks of various shades. The winner takes all, just like elsewhere in our increasingly competitive and instrumentalist world.

Twenty-five years have passed since the fall of the Berlin Wall and the collapse of communism in Europe. Much time has elapsed and much has changed in Europe beyond recognition. Therefore, it is quite legitimate to ask: where are we now? And what is to be done?

Let me start by saying that one of the paradoxes of political change is that the less power you have, the more committed – in the moral and political sense – you can be. Eastern European dissidents have never exploited hatred and fear, those two precious commodities of modern politics. Instead, they have stressed responsibility for humanity and commitment to human rights. Self-victimization, deliberate and joyful powerlessness, wilful disengagement, celebration of one's own victimhood, and comparative martyrology with its question of who is suffering the most – as if one person's suffering could be weighed against another's – were still to come.

Twenty-five years after the fall of communism, we are tempted to exploit our victimhood as an aspect of foreign policy: as soon as we don't have power, then powerlessness and suffering becomes the passport to the Heaven of Global Attention. Sometimes we even go as far as explaining away our political failures and the low points of recent history as something that inevitably arises from our powerlessness or the infinite manipulations around us. Although it appears to be quite a trendy manoeuvre in power games nowadays, which allows us to gain more moral legitimacy by getting more attention for our increased suffering and power-lessness, things were very different in the days when communism was defeated.

By and large, this is an awkward trend in present Eastern and Central Europe, since it springs from a global tendency to seek attention at any cost in exchange for popularity, publicity and power. Heart-breaking stories, abandonment of privacy, and self-exposure have become the means to achieve prestige and power for those who can perform the high art of translation of the private into the public, making their personal and intimate stories a public property or even breaking news – an art now in great demand. Normally, this is a function of celebrities, although intellectuals and politicians cannot survive other than by becoming celebrities or victims, as you, Zygmunt, have noticed in your books.

Whatever the case, things were not like this twenty-five years ago. Eastern and Central Europe became famous for its fearless-ness and engagement, rather than its fear and disengagement. The Solidarity movement in Poland, the very climax of Eastern and Central European courage and the sporadic powers of association, was anticipated by the Helsinki groups in the former USSR, the Memorial group dissidents in Russia, and other units of dissenting minds and nay-sayers. In those days, almost nobody spoke about suffering and victimhood, as people were concerned with how to win back their sense of self-worth, dignity and self-confidence.

Needless to say, we are talking here about rather small groups of fearless individuals; yet it was they who made it possible to smash communism from the face of Europe by translating their individual courage into popular fervour, and also into a strong belief in the right cause. Courage, instead of fear and hatred, was behind the miracle of Eastern and Central Europe's liberty, both in the Annus Mirabilis of 1989, and in the years of dissent that preceded and anticipated the liberation and emancipation of Yet Another Europe, as it was called by Czesław Miłosz and Milan Kundera. This especially stood in sharp contrast with the hatred and fear that were thoroughly exploited by the Soviet regime and its satellites as a means of political mobilization and social control of the masses.

Contempt for fear is deeply grounded in Eastern and Central European thought and politics of dissent and freedom. If we are to grant George Orwell the title of Honorary Eastern European, as the Russian poetess and dissident Natalya Gorbanevskaya strongly suggested we should do, his *1984* also exposes this characteristically Eastern European moral concern. The main character of *1984*, Winston Smith, and his lover Julia, despise fear, which they try hard to confront and eliminate from themselves.

Before George Orwell's dystopia, written in 1948, Mikhail Bulgakov, in *The Master and Margarita*, depicted fear as the source of evil. According to him, fear is the reason for betrayal of a friend, our disloyalty to and rejection of a mentor, our amoral failure to take responsibility for a human individual's life, even if she or he has established eye contact with us and captivated our attention and imagination. Fear is what Pontius Pilate despises in himself the most after he washes his hands and allows Joshua (the name of Jesus Christ in Bulgakov's masterpiece, which is deeply influenced by Manichaeism and Ernest Renan's version of the history of Christianity) to be crucified.

Eastern Europe fulfilled the silent promises and moral obligations of its towering thinkers and eminent writers by overcoming hatred and fear. In 1989, communism fell in Eastern Europe as a consequence of courage, resolve, fearlessness and solidarity. To reiterate a subtle point made by Michael Ignatieff, the human rights discourse was the outcome of Eastern courage and Western organization. How ironic that some politicians and public figures in present-day Eastern Europe tend to describe human rights solely as a West European invention with which the West supposedly control us, imposing on us its 'alien' values of secularism and respect for minorities. This is especially the case when it comes to defending ludicrous legislation on what are called 'traditional values' or 'genuine family', or other pearls of homophobic and anti-European wisdom.

What happened to us? Milan Kundera wrote in his essay 'The Tragedy of Central Europe' that all Central European revolts and revolutions were essentially romantic, nostalgic and, in effect, conservative and anachronistic.[1] Out of our idealization of Europe, especially its early modernity, we firmly identified freedom and democracy with Europe, shaping our emancipation policies as a return to Europe. We thought with good reason that the Soviet version of modernity was the most brutal one, and, therefore, we sought to replace it with Europe – yet a problem was that the kind of Europe we envisaged and identified ourselves with did not exist at the time of our upheavals. It did not become any better or worse – it simply became something radically different from what we imagined and thought it would and should be.

Our velvet and singing revolutions were about how to arrest social change. Yet we ourselves became hostages of rapid social and political change transforming our part of Europe into a laboratory for a historically unprecedented acceleration of history, with its uncertainties and insecurities. For example, over the past twenty-five years, more than half a million people have left Lithuania, settling in the USA, the UK, Ireland, Spain, Germany or elsewhere. This is hardly a specifically Lithuanian phenomenon, as Poland and Slovakia are facing similar challenges. Striking social divisions and endemic corruption frequently led Eastern Europeans to disenchantment, even with what were their most impressive achievements, including their accession to the EU.

And here comes a pivotal point. Populism came to our countries, firmly establishing itself as a major political trajectory. What is populism then? Is it a genuine concern with the well-being of the nation expressed in an exaggerated form of patriotism? In fact, it is not, since the real substance of this phenomenon lies elsewhere. Populism is a skilled and masterful translation of the private into the public, with an additional ability to exploit fear to the full. Fear and hatred are twin sisters, as we know quite well. One never walks alone, without the other.

Yet this time it is not organized hatred, as in Orwell's Two Minutes Hate, or a séance of collective hysteria and group orgy of hatred, as orchestrated by the Party and practised in the Soviet

Union and other People's Democracies. Instead, it is the real fear of a private person elevated to the rank of public concern, or sometimes translated even into mass obsession.

The question arises of what this is fear of? The answer is quite simple: it is fear of anyone who comes to personify our own insecurities and uncertainties, whose facial features determine the first and last names we call them thanks to excessive sensationalist media coverages, tabloid editorials and conspiracy theories. It is fear of Islam and Muslims, fear of immigrants, fear of gays and lesbians, fear of godless pinkos, fear of new Jewish world conspiracies. You name it.

As Mark Lilla shows in his acute analysis of France after the Charlie Hebdo tragedy, Michel Houellebecq's new novel, *Soumission*, has become a potent tool in the hands of the Far Right, instead of serving his primary and major purposes as a dystopian writer, provocateur, polemicist and satirist – the way he was until now.[2] In a society of fear, laughter runs the risk of becoming a war cry, and satire, like all novels of warning, tends to be translated into gloomy political pamphlets of fear and hate.

We became the kind of Europe that we thought would never accept us as part of it. We adopted all its phobias and stereotypes, which earlier worked against us. Or the world has become a Global Single Eastern and Central Europe. If that is the case, the change could be irreversible.

Zygmunt Bauman You write: 'truth is success, and, conversely, success is truth'. And add: 'The winner takes all.' This strikes me as true, and nothing but... But is it the *whole* truth about truth? Far from it.

To start with I guess we need to spell out the hidden premise lying behind your statements: 'Truth' is an agonistic notion; a notion that belongs to the vocabulary of antagonism, combat, contest, conflict, struggle. Whenever the idea of 'truth' appears in discourse, it signals the presence of contesters, competitors, detractors: it is their opposition that calls for – necessitates? – its entry. In an unlikely condition of universal agreement, the notion of truth would be redundant. Were that bizarre condition universal eternally, the birth of such notion would have been inconceivable.

'Truth' in the singular is, paradoxically, an oblique testimony to its plurality. The assertion '*This* is true' derives its sense from

being paired, inseparably, with an assertion '*That* is untrue.' It
therefore assumes/asserts/confirms latently what it manifestly
denies. Or perhaps it is a declaration of war on its own origin: on
the state of affairs that has brought it, complete with its need, into
being. That state of affairs is marked by the plurality of mind-sets,
standpoints, opinions and beliefs. Being true, or 'being in the
right', is and cannot but be a stake in the rivalry between plurali-
ties of irreconcilable – or refusing to be reconciled – claims. Such
plurality is an inescapable, and so in all probability ineradicable,
consequence of the diversity of human modes of being-in-the-
world (also ineradicable, as well as irreparable, I believe). In other
words: 'Truth' belongs to the big family of (in Whitehead's terminology) 'essentially contested concepts'.

To go on – that family is indeed large and incessantly expand-
ing. The characteristic feature of the contest to which all and each
of its members are subjected is the compression of the descriptive
and the axiological – or rather subjection of *rei* to *aestimationis*
in the search for *adequatio*. Here are just two off-the-cuff illustrations of that general rule: exactly the same behavioural syndrome
may be dubbed as the mark of an innovator and trail-blazer, or
of a botcher and trouble-maker; the same kinds of deeds may be
denominated as the acts of terrorists or of freedom-fighters. And
they are – all too commonly. Or consider the difference between
an act of violence and an act of law-enforcement. Would a visitor
from outer space, armed with all our sense organs yet unaware of
our value hierarchies, tell one from the other?

And so we confront one more quandary – yet deeper, yet more
mind-boggling, and yet further away from a 'universally agreed'
solution, even though it has worried philosophers and kept them
busy for centuries. If one can try with some success to set apart
the truth and a lie in the space of *rei*, is one able, or even entitled,
to attempt the same in the realm 'of *aestimationes*? Isn't the
expression 'false value' an oxymoron? How would you proceed
to 'prove' or 'falsify' a value, and what sort of authority, if any,
would the outcome of your procedure carry in a truth-contest? I
am repeating here questions asked since ancient times, albeit we
are still as incapable of answering them as was Pontius Pilate, and
still waiting for Jesus Christ's binding answer. To be sure, answers
on offer abound – but none has thus far managed to escape the
'essentially contested status': not in the realm of philosophical

discourse; and, more importantly yet, not in the realm of human practice either. Nowhere is it evident as starkly as in collective memory – and so also in the 'politics of history' that feeds and thrives on its endemic deficiencies and vulnerabilities.

Each variety of collective memory is, and can't but be, selective – it is, however, the current or aspiring politicians of history who guide the selection. It's not only that, as you say, 'success is truth'. Political success means the capability to overhaul historical memory (starting with renaming city streets and squares, rewriting school textbooks and replacing public monuments) – which in turn renders politics successful, or at least is hoped to do so. It is the victors who write history, as Winston Churchill allegedly suggested. It would, however, be more correct to say that history is continually *rewritten* by *successive* victors; and that the victors' staying in the power they won is the necessary – even if not necessarily sufficient – condition of their narrative's immunity to a next, and a next-but-one, rewriting. A temporary immunity – always temporary, to be sure. 'For in the world in which we live it is no longer merely a question of the decay of collective memory and declining consciousness of the past, but of the aggressive [assault on] whatever memory remains, the deliberate distortion of the historical record, the invention of mythological pasts in the service of the powers of darkness.'[3] It is the endemic pliability and short life-expectation of historical memory that tempt and allow 'the victors' to resort to those unscrupulous assaults with a well-grounded expectation of winning. As Henry A. Giroux comments, just a few years after the catastrophic Iraq escapade, in a sharp, short, yet shocking recent study – a must-read for everybody seriously interested in the current state of the 'politics of history' game:

> The current mainstream debate regarding the crisis in Iraq and Syria offers a near perfect example of both the death of historical memory and the collapse of critical thinking in the United States. It also signifies the emergence of a profoundly anti-democratic culture of manufactured ignorance and social indifference. Surely, historical memory is under assault when the dominant media give airtime to the incessant war mongering of politicians such as Senators John McCain and Lindsay Graham and retro pundits such as Bill Kristol, Douglas Feith, Condoleezza Rice and Paul Wolfowitz – not one of whom has any credibility given how they have worked

to legitimate the unremitting web of lies and deceit that provided cover for the disastrous US invasion of Iraq under the Bush/Cheney administration.[4]

Giroux ascribed to the present-day hegemony of the 'culture of illiteracy' a great deal of responsibility for the unprecedented facility with which lies, inventions and artificially contrived public amnesia manipulate (or just efface) the contents of public historical awareness, repeating after John Pilger that what is at work in the death of literacy and the promotion of ignorance as a civic virtue is a 'confidence trick' in which 'the powerful would like us to believe that we live in an eternal present in which reflection is limited to Facebook, and historical narrative is the preserve of Hollywood'.[5] Soundbites replace narrative, shallowness replaces depth, and surfing amidst flotsam and jetsam of the past replaces reflection. We live in a culture of forgetting, not memorizing. Nowadays, the stockbrokers (simultaneously stakeholders) of historical memory focus their efforts on eroding its powers of retention and promoting historical amnesia.

I will make two more comments on two other important issues you raise. One is treachery, which has chased out fidelity, that adhesive once used to cement/integrate human identities. Again, this phenomenon chimes well with the rest of liquid-modern culture, prominent as it is for devaluing duration and ennobling transience and promoting 'flexibility' to the rank of the paramount skill in the art of *savoir-vivre*. In lieu of the Sartrean 'projet de la vie', a weather-vane is nowadays recommended as the supreme (perhaps the only reliable and trustworthy) guide in the self-identification venture – commended precisely for its capability of promptly recording the slightest change in the current fashions, fads and foibles, as well as in the current 'talk of the town' and 'the only game in town' currently played. This sort of counsel so harmoniously in tune with the drowning man's habit of clutching at a straw is – isn't it? – only what could be expected from a hurried life lived under Thomas Hylland Eriksen's 'tyranny of the moment' and the pressure of Stephen Bertman's 'nowist culture', David Harvey's time/space compression or Paul Virilio's speed/space – with all solid orientation points (including the heritage and bequests of the past) put on castors, lighthouses replaced by blinking strobes (from the Greek word for 'whirling', 'gyral' or 'vertiginous'), and the avatars of Baroness Orczy's Scarlet Pimpernel substituted for fellow travellers. I suggest that what Reason, in alliance with experience and empirical evidence, prompts us to do in order to make sense of contempory men's and women's lives, is to substitute the concept of 'the unstoppable process of reidentification' for the zombie-term 'identity'. In this case, as in so many others, the managers of politics, in cahoots with consumer markets, capitalize on the liquid-modern giddiness of the human existential condition and the uncertainties it so massively generates.

And one last issue picked from the many you've discussed: the cruel plight visited upon the children of the East European string of revolutions by the leap to freedom a quarter-century ago: 'the kind of Europe we envisaged and identified ourselves with did not exist at the time of our upheavals'. I leave aside the moot question of whether it *ever* existed – as the central point here is the inclination, common to all radical revolutions, to patch together the vision of the destination out of the resentment felt to things vexing and repellent in the *status quo ante*; each radical revolution risks for that reason a great number of diverse collateral casualties, victims of frustrated hopes and stillborn expectations. Not unexpectedly, therefore, revolutions stand all-too-often accused of the sin, or crime, of *infanticide*. There is some truth in this charge, though it often serves as a cover-up device for the more important, indeed seminal, truth that (victorious) revolutions tend to multiply the ranks of their self-appointed children who try *a posteriori* to revise their pedigree through gathering/inventing proofs of their *ex-post-facto* chosen parentage. My main point, however, is that an unduly neglected while much more significant and consequential, trait of revolutions is their *parricidal* tendency. At any rate, the tendency of the emergent political elite of post-revolutionary society to disarm, debunk and denigrate the fathers of the revolution, their undesirable competitors for public respect and authority, goes a long way towards making sense of the last quarter-century of Polish political history – as it does, I guess, of its Lithuanian counterpart. Or am I wrong?

LD Nothing could be nearer the truth than your idea of its highly ambivalent and agonistic nature. I take it here not as 'truth' in the Durkheimian sense but, instead, as truth about the truth itself. In fact, we are longing for agonistic concepts that keep us mobilized, resilient and ready to confront the disturbing complexities of modern life. It is precisely for these reasons that we so desperately need 'faith', 'identity' and 'community', whether walking in the guise of anonymous affirmations of our lives and actions or as masks of social ritual.

Along similar lines, I find myself thinking that the nineteenth century was the time when the new collective actors on the political map of the world emerged. True, after the First World War, new nation-states came into existence, but the second half of the nineteenth century paved the way for this new civilization-shaping movement. The period was called the nation-building century, and also the era of the springtime of the peoples. What happened after the Second World War was perceived as a turning point in world history in terms of providing the closing page in the political saga of modern Europe. The nations were born, the state borders drawn, and nobody believed that we could step into the same river twice. Nay, nobody even suspected that we would change our historical-political time zone.

For a long time, we took it for granted that we were living in an increasingly post-national world. The fall of the Berlin Wall indicated the end of the modern bloody history of opposing ideologies, as proposed by Francis Fukuyama. The blow dealt to Europe by a horrible war in the Former Yugoslavia was twofold: first and foremost, it exposed the impotence, self-inflicted moral and political blindness, and self-deception of all Europe's politics and soft power which culminated in Srebrenica with 8,000 civilians killed in two days before the eyes of Dutch peacekeeping forces – far and away the most horrible crime against humanity in Europe since the Second World War; second, it revealed the ease with which people jumped fifty years back in time arriving in a radically different historical-political time zone.

A most horrifying thing in Bosnia-Herzegovina was that people were slaughtering each other with names and labels on their lips that had absolutely nothing to do with what should have been seen as the present reality. Such labels as *Chetniks* (Serbian nationalists and monarchists) and *Ustashi* (Croatian fascists) came back to reality as soon as there was a need to justify a new slaughter in a fratricidal war. Were there any real *Chetniks* and *Ustashi* in the Former Yugoslavia in the 1990s? Of course, there were none.

Unfortunately, the EU then lived in its own historical-political time zone – which was that of a fairy-tale, to reiterate a witty remark once made by Pascal Bruckner during a talk in Bratislava.

What happened in the Former Yugoslavia, then, was that disturbed or politically troubled individuals withdrew from reality, choosing to live temporarily in a radically different historical-political time zone and to re-enact it. They chose to live elsewhere, withdrawing from social reality and abandoning it for the sake of a phantom, a short-term logocratic project, a spectre of selective memory and wilful forgetting. And what about the *déjà-vu* feeling we get on hearing and reading the label of 'Banderites' exploited by Russian state-sponsored propaganda? Are there any flesh-and-blood Banderites in Kyiv today? Were they there a year ago during the Euromaidan Revolution?

In fact, there is a long way to go from plain brainwashing and propaganda to the more complex phenomenon of withdrawal from the present time zone and eventual return to it. What lies behind this mechanism is historical trauma, a suppressed pattern of identity, or conflict of identities and loyalties. We may cease explaining reality as it is and, instead, may switch to the past trying to re-enact or recover it. Hence, there have been countless memory wars in Europe. The withdrawal-and-return form of existence can therefore be seen not only in the case of adiaphorization of consciousness (abandoning and leaving the zone of our human sensitivity temporarily, and then returning to it), but in troubled historical-political time zones as well.

Deep discontent with the present time and the resulting temptation to repeat or re-enact history are among the most explosive and dangerous feelings and conditions in our world. What results from them is the loss of the sense of social and political time. Dictators – or even perfectly reasonable individuals with, one would think, unquestionable democratic credentials – may think that they can deliver justice or derive it from the past, projecting it onto the present or the future. Yet not every form of withdrawal-and-return poses a grave danger to the world.

In his novel *The Winter of Our Discontent* (1961), John Steinbeck exposed this mechanism as deeply embedded in the modern pattern of human behaviour: we may vacate the realm of norms and part with our views and attitudes of today for the sake of well-being, self-esteem, safety, and security tomorrow. He describes, with the stroke of genius, this mechanism of living elsewhere temporarily for the sake of regaining or re-enacting control over circumstances. To be able to reshape our lives, we have to retreat from ourselves in terms of our attitudes, long-term commitments, value-and-idea orientations, and even sensitivities.

This is even more true with regard to the realm of nations. Nationalism has long been regarded by sociologists as a specific phenomenon of the nineteenth century, and rightly so. However, this fact itself does not mean that nations cannot be reshaped or that they cannot intensify their daily plebiscite, as Ernest Renan would have had it.[6] Nations may come into existence repeatedly, one more time, withdrawing from our postmodern reality and celebrating a set of sentiments and attitudes that sociologists would ascribe to the second half of the nineteenth century or the first half of the twentieth.

In fact, during the war in the Former Yugoslavia, individuals, groups and societies actively re-enacted and relived the periods of pre- and post-war European history. It may well be suggested that Ukraine lives now in its own historical-political time zone, formed by critical junctures of their modern history and politics enabling and repeating similar – or even identical – moral choices to those made in the twentieth century. When Angela Merkel noticed that Vladimir Putin lives elsewhere in terms of political reality, she may have felt his disconnectedness from her own historical-political time zone.

The twenty-first century dramatically encountered the nineteenth and twentieth centuries, with some grim flashbacks of Europe's fairly recent political history. Linear history exists neither in Europe nor beyond it. Human beings and societies are doomed to dwell in different time zones. Can such a historical-political time zone, as well as our withdrawal-and-return mechanism, be described as cognitive phenomena? Are they related to our self-indulgent and selective memory? Or is it more about our indispensable moral choices, as moralists would tend to insist? Whatever the case, this shows that linear and progressive history is an unfulfilled promise of modernity – just like social progress in general. Universalism is part of that same failed project – but this is still to come, along with my insights into what happened to Eastern Europe.

ZB Myths of origin (and the mothballed memories you unravel belong to that category) are not records of historical events. They are rather scenarios for plays meant to be re-enacted over and over again, with each re-staging carrying perhaps a different ending, yet following a similar pattern and so rolling the otherwise linear time into a circular one. They clasp together the idea of a preordained order of things with a call to action: to complete the predesigned circle, the pattern needs to be followed to its pre-described end. The birth of a national community is an irreversible, no-appeal-allowed accomplishment, yet also an unfinished (unfinishable?) process – a beginning of a never-ending and never-broken string of re-births; this is one of the messages – I guess the main message – of Renan's reference to the day-in, day-out plebiscite. The message is: the ballot is not a one-off event; the ballot box needs to be refilled day in, day out. Myths of origin – foundational or etiological myths – wed continuous action to a preordained duty. For Johann-Gottlieb Fichte, Germans were born German, yet the meaning of being German was to live one's life in the uniquely German way. Auguste-Maurice Barrès would voice a similar opinion about the French-ness of the French. Belonging to a national community is an indomitable, and so indisputable, fate that also sets its children free – though their freedom can take no other form than embracing that preordained fate with gratitude and dedication.

It is tempting to view that 'nation- [and state-] building century', which you invoke, as the time of recycling the centuries-old model of the God vs Man relation (God bringing Man to life, Man's duty to dedicate his life, in exchange, to His service) into the Nation vs Man liaison, culminating, in the 'Spring of Nations' in 1848, in recycling the anointed royalty's hereditary rights to rule into the ultimate authority of the 'people' or 'Volk', and spawning by the end of the nineteenth century in Europe the first series of 'Nation-States' – a pattern later to be exported to the rest of the continents by Europe-centred colonial empires and emulated by former colonies after their dissolution, as well as elevated by Woodrow Wilson in Versailles to the rank of the universal right of nations to self-determination.

In my view, the Augsburg conference of Europe's ruling dynasties, convoked in 1555 to put an end to the devastating post-Reformation religious war, served as a take-off point for that process. The formula 'cuius regio eius religio' designed for that purpose in Augsburg – and finally accepted after another thirty-year-long war (1617–48) by another conference held simultaneously in Münster and Osnabrück and grudgingly put into operation thereafter – was to provide the pattern for the territorially sovereign nation-states (with 'natio' being gradually, yet unflinchingly, substituted for 'religio'). The Austro-Hungarian Empire ('the only empire that is recalled with nostalgia in all its former territories', as Eric Hobsbawm commented)[7] was the only part of Europe that resisted the application of this formula, transferring the phenomenon of nationhood from politics to culture and promoting thereby, and practising, its decoupling from the idea of territorial sovereignty. That rule-defying practice served Otto Bauer, Friedrich Rainer and Vladimir Medem as the source of inspiration for their visions of 'cultural autonomy' of nations replacing the model of their territorial separation and political sovereignty – following the example of the coterminous trend to separate the Church from the State. That vision was laid in the grave together with the Austro-Hungary that inspired and attempted to implement it.

Well, we are *not* living in a 'post-national' world. Far from it – the 'century of nation-building' seems interminably long; its end is nowhere in sight. Paradoxically, it was the unstoppable globalization of human interdependence and of power – which set the options for individual and collective life-choices – that boosted the recovery of nation-building ardour and stamina at the moment when, by the majority opinion, they were already running out of steam. Retrospectively, we may gather that this resurrection and restoration of nation-building zeal was precisely what could and should have been expected, in view of the progressive erosion of the self-same territorial sovereignty whose vision it originally triggered, invigorated and guided. Territorial sovereignty is already in many respects an illusion. All three legs of the tripod on which it used to be perched – economic, military and cultural self-sufficiency – are nowadays rickety and teetering: indeed, a fiction. The League of Nations had 42 members at its foundation, and 23 at the moment of its dissolution. The United Nations had 53 members at its foundation, and currently boasts 193. These numbers and their dynamics convey a clear message: the quantity of formally sovereign territorial states is growing (and in all probability will continue to grow) as the idea of sovereignty turns eerie and ever more phantom-like. It is ever more easy nowadays to claim independence and acquire its recognition, as the test that the claimants need to pass to be granted independent status is becoming less and less demanding, and as the characteristics shared by the governments of old and newly composed states alike are a fairly limited remit and potency. For all intents and practices, the role of state government is reduced to an aggrandized and ennobled version of local police precincts burdened with responsibility for supervising and preserving the rule of law and order within the boundaries of their locality. And as the strings attached to the ambitions become weaker or are completely severed, the temptation to join the long line of nation-states-in-waiting stretches yet longer. Let me quote Eric Hobsbawm's early – laconic, pithy and witty – warning of where the present trend may lead:

> Any speck in the Pacific can look forward to independence and a good time for its president, if it happens to possess a location for a naval base for which more solvent states will compete, a lucky gift of nature such as manganese, or merely enough beaches and pretty girls to become a tourist paradise [...] The majority of the members of the UN is soon likely to consist of the late twentieth century (republican) equivalents to Saxe-Coburg-Gotha and Schwarzburg-Sonderhausen [...] If the Seychelles can have a vote in the UN as good as Japan's [...] then surely only the sky is the limit for the Isle of Man or the Channel Islands.[8]

And let me remind you of another, no less grave – if not yet graver – factor (no joking here!), which Hobsbawm added a few years later: for the multinationals, 'the ideal world is one of no states, or at least of small rather than larger states [...] Unless it has oil, the smaller the state, the weaker it is, and the less money it takes to buy a government.'[9]

LD Let us pity poor nationalism. All the calamities of the twentieth century are blamed on it. Yet an attempt to explain the twentieth century's social catastrophes without attributing them to the decline of empires, changed power constellations, and the totalitarian 'modernization' of the world, but, instead, attributing them to nationalism is, at the very least unfair, and perhaps even foolish. The two world wars were not started by nationalism, but by collapsing empires, and the new regimes stepping into their place, which sought to occupy the former power positions and realize the same totalitarian projects, regimes guided by global communist and racist Nazi ideologies.

Moreover, empires have collapsed thanks to nationalism. It was due to the disintegration of the Russian Empire that Poland, Finland and the Baltic States became independent – Finland at that stage was also considered a Baltic State. The British Empire was seriously shaken by the battles for Irish liberation, while Mahatma Gandhi's movement had an impact no less profound. The last nail in the coffin of the French Empire was the war in Algeria.

This raises the simple question: where should our sympathies lie? With the nations who have liberated themselves from empires (sometimes these empires were quite liberal – for example, the Austro-Hungarian Empire – but empires nonetheless) or with the fallen regimes? Whose side are we on – that of imperialism or that of freedom? The burden of the white man or the emancipation of former colonies? Those who secretly believe in the post-imperialistic vision of a mission that instils a civilized way of life or the legitimacy of new nations of the world?

The belief that great powers stabilize the world, which is why they should not be dismantled, is truly absurd. This logic led to the outbreak of both world wars and is most likely to ignite another, if there is no timely reaction to declarations that the collapse of the Soviet Union was the greatest geopolitical catastrophe of the twentieth century. In fact, this statement by Vladimir Putin – the long-term, or simply recurrent, president of Russia – is different from the expression of post-imperialist syndrome in the countries of Western Europe – unlike Western politicians, Russia's president did not even try to disguise his way of speaking and thinking.

What is being discussed is not a political façade, which needs to serve as a reminder of the power that was formerly held, but is now lost, but the restoration of the Soviet Union and the borders of the former empires. The world may well be better off if Russia would only apply Western post-imperialism, especially the British version that allowed the 'English', with their trademark political humour and ability to laugh at their former pretences and grandeur, to bid farewell to their imperial past.

When the tragedy of the Former Yugoslavia is mentioned, and nationalism is offered as an explanation, it is hard to dismiss the thought that a helplessly superficial perspective on the problem is being adopted. The Balkans were a ticking time bomb immediately after the collapse of the Austro-Hungarian Empire. It is obvious that after the Second World War this fragmented country was superficially brought together as a federation by Josip Broz Tito, thereby only conserving Pandora's box, which was bound to open up sooner or later.

It was not nationalism, but the delayed domino effect of the collapse of empires, that created massacres in places where the West could have and should have intervened in time but failed to do so. There is no bloodier period in international politics than the first and last phases of an imperial cycle – it is the formation and collapse of empires that start a long-term effect of killing and destruction; yet in their periods of stability, they can undertake their 'civilizing mission' in the colonies and maintain a period of relative political stability based on the balance of power.

In this respect, aren't there uncanny similarities between the massacres in Yugoslavia and in Rwanda? In both cases, one group was favoured at the cost of the other, which naturally sowed the seeds of their mutual deadly hate: Belgian bureaucrats and administrators chose the Tutsis, not the Hutus, to work in the police force or as minor clerks. In both cases, the passivity of the West, merely waiting to see how it would all end, was in itself a crime. And in both cases, the empires finally collapsed, and in their former colonies an artificial code of ethnic and political relations was introduced. The real threat is the delayed collapse of old empires and the resulting formation of new hegemonic derivatives. I do not wish to make allusions, but it may well be that the real and most terrible effects of the disintegration of the Soviet Union will only be felt in the possibly not-too-distant future.

Here we find ourselves in the world of modernity and ambivalence. Everything depends on the social and political context. Like marriage, nationalism can easily become a tool of oppression or of emancipation, traditionalism or reform, subjugation or liberation. Like the search for an identity, nationalism and patriotism come as a promise of self-comprehension and self-fulfilment in the world of ambivalence and ambiguity. Yet, if we end up as a conservative nationalist opposed to a liberal patriot, or vice versa, we cannot find a way out of this predicament.

In fact, some cases of nationalism were successful and far-reaching in terms of their implications for European thought and action, as well as for its politics and culture. Needless to say, nationalism comes in many guises, from conservative and liberal to exclusionary and radical. Yet some of them seem to have had their universalistic programmes and aspirations, for example French or American nationalism, usually taken as civic-minded and opposed to the German form, that is, an ethnic-minded and *Volk*-spirited sort of nationalism. As Louis Dumont described this phenomenon in his study *Homo Aequalis, II: L'idéologie allemande, France–Allemagne et retour* (1976): 'J'ai ainsi contrasté le Français: "Je suis homme par nature et français par accident", et l'Allemand: "Je suis essentiellement un Allemand, et je suis un homme grâce à ma qualité d'Allemand"' ('I have contrasted the French person – "I am a human being by nature, and French by accident" – and the German: "I am essentially German, and I am a human being due to my trait of being German"').[10]

We were tempted to believe that exclusionary and illiberal nationalism was more of an Eastern and Central European phenomenon and problem, which may have been true two decades ago. Yet, on closer examination, it appears that the spectre of nationalism is out haunting again – especially in the Old Europe, rather than in the New, in Donald Rumsfeld's parlance. Just recall what happened during the 2014 elections to the European Parliament.

'We are coming', said Nigel Farage, the leader of UKIP (United Kingdom Independence Party) and Co-Chair of the Europe of Freedom and Democracy group in the European Parliament. As if to say that this is now his time, Farage came up with the punchline directed straight at Martin Schulz, President of the European Parliament: 'Please don't pretend that nothing has happened. You know perfectly well that it has. And the day is nigh when all your EU institutions will be plain dead. We are coming.' I am paraphrasing his words, yet I can vouch for its credibility and content.

So the message is clear – if we are to believe the most theatrical and eloquent political clown I have seen during the past five years that I spent as his fellow Member of the European Parliament (2009–14), that's the beginning of the end of the EU. Needless to say, the news about the death of the EU is slightly exaggerated, to paraphrase Mark Twain. The Centre Right and Left will outweigh an increasingly visible minority of the Far Right led by Marine Le Pen and Nigel Farage. When the time comes, conventional and pro-European groups will always achieve a decisive and crucial majority over pivotal issues in the EU.

Yet on one point we have to agree with Nigel Farage regardless. The 2014 elections to the European Parliament did make a difference. We cannot pretend any longer that Far Right voices and Eurosceptics are still a tiny minority that is easily relegated to the margins of EU politics. The shocking success of UKIP in the UK (27 per cent of votes) was coupled with the triumph of Le Front National (FN) in France (a quarter of all votes). Alongside genuine fascist parties – such as Greece's Golden Dawn, and Hungary's Jobbik – the Far Right and anti-immigration parties – such as UKIP, FN and Geert Wilders' Party of Freedom in the Netherlands – will make up quite a noisy minority of around 140 voices in the newly elected European Parliament.

First and foremost, these forces are not only strongly anti-EU– they are essentially anti-European and overtly pro-Kremlin. We only have to recall them praising Vladimir Putin to the skies as a supposed defender of conservative, family and traditional values, which allowed Farage and Marine Le Pen to close ranks with Jobbik – a wretched and disgraceful alliance, to say the least. Farage was even more self-revealing when, in one of his recent interviews, he went as far as suggesting that two grave mistakes made by the EU were the adoption of the euro and allowing the accession of Eastern European countries to the EU, giving them new social mobility and dignity (and permitting them not to be embarrassed anymore by Western European immigration officers with their intrusive questions and poorly concealed disdain for Eastern Europe, I would add).

However tempting it may be, we cannot reduce the entire analysis of the 2014 elections to the European Parliament to moral outrage. True, it is something like a heavy hangover and a wake-up call for the EU, yet this is the right time to find the answer to the question: what happened? The 2014 elections should have served as a wake-up call and a reminder that Euroscepticism is far from a *force majeure* or natural disaster – instead, it is a collective sentiment of European citizens skilfully exploited by populist parties and translated into a war-cry, a quasi-programme, and a pseudo-vision of the future. It is enough to beat the drums of threat and portray the EU as a spectre of velvet totalitarianism or else to demonize Brussels, and behold the mandate – you can win the elections to the despised European Parliament, an institution which Mr. Farage hates and holds in contempt, even refusing to attend committee meetings, yet this does not prevent him from being well paid by it. No programme or vision is needed – just an imagined monster onto which you project all your discontents and worries, caused by modern politics and life.

While the former USSR – with its ideological charms and deceptive, seductive powers that captivated much of Europe and Latin America – seems to have been a Shakespearean tragedy, today's Russia appears to be a farce. It is a mafia state and a banal kleptocracy, instead of the former Jerusalem of the Proletariat or the proud heir of the Enlightenment project. The former USSR was able to fool millions of ambitious and dissenting minds, whereas Vladimir Putin's Russia is capable of casting a spell on the Far Right – the new symbolic and actual allies of the Kremlin now appear to be the xenophobes, racists, antisemites and homophobes of Europe – such as Marine Le Pen and her like – instead of the folks of Lion Feuchtwanger's or Jean-Paul Sartre's cut.

Is this a sort of *coup de grâce* dealt to Russia as a successor state of the former USSR? Is it a recurrent failure of modernization in a huge part of Eastern Europe related to what the Russian historian Yuri Afanasiev has described as the matrix of Russia's unchangeability? Or is it a broader historical-political cycle of a civilization-shaping movement in Eastern Europe? The way in which Vytautas Kavolis describes the former Soviet Union as a failed project of modernization, and communism as a rival civilization, is, in a way, reminiscent of Raymond Aron, Alain Besançon, Ernest Gellner, Leszek Kołakowski, Czesław Miłosz and you, too, Zygmunt:

> The Soviet Union has for seventy years endeavored to produce a new civilization by establishing a secular version of the religion-above-culture paradigm as its center. The result was a pattern most similar, among contemporary civilizations, to that of the Islamic world, except that (1) a *secular* religion was placed in the position of super-ordination to all culture, and (2) this secular religion was, in contrast to Islam, not deeply embedded in the attitudes of the 'masses' or the 'intellectual elites'. It therefore has remained an

artificial entity, not a 'genuine civilization' capable of attracting adherence even without the use of violence; a failed effort in a boundary region of the West to become a civilizational alternative to it. ... This pattern has now collapsed. But will Eastern Europe move toward the modern West, in which ontological hierarchy has been replaced, beginning in the seventeenth century, by a polymorphous political-moral-aesthetic polylogue as the main integrative device? Or will Eastern Europe remain a culturally distinctive region, with another, perhaps more 'traditionalist', ontological hierarchy acquiring hegemony?[11]

To tell you the truth, I find myself increasingly sceptical about the necessity to draw a sharp dividing line between Central and Eastern Europe in terms of human rights records and fidelity to liberal-democratic sensibilities. Whereas Viktor Orbán's regime appears to be a soft version of Putinism, which is a blow to Hungarian democracy, Miloš Zeman's tirades support Vladimir Putin and blast the legacy of Václav Havel as damaging the economy of the region (true, defence of human rights can work against trade agreements and strategic economic partnerships). It is hardly an inspiring, or even consoling, picture.

Ernest Gellner, in a posthumously published essay on how to rethink and write history at the end of the twentieth century, depicts the collapse of communism as a disaster. There must be a moral order provided by a civilization. According to Gellner,

> The manner of the dismantling of the Russian revolution may come to be seen as a disaster comparable only with the revolution itself. I do not wish to be misunderstood. I write as a life-long anti-communist and anti-Marxist. For a person of my age and background, I belong to what sometimes felt like a small minority of people who never passed through a Marxist phase. ... Yet I deplore the disintegration of the Soviet Union; not because I ever sympathized with the ideology which had inspired it, but because of concerns about the need for continuity. Marxism had provided the societies under its sway with a moral order – a set of moral values which helped people to orient themselves. They knew what the rules, the idiom and the slogans were. These added up to a system you could understand and adjust to, whether or not you approved of it. An east European living under communism who confronted a person from the free world had a measure of dignity: deprived of many civil liberties, and a western standard of living, he

nevertheless belonged to a rival civilization – one which stood for something different. It had not been doing very well, by its own standards or by most others. But that had not always been obvious and no single individual had been personally dishonored by the historic mistakes which had led to communism. Today, a typical east European is simply a very poor cousin. If he is an intellectual, his best prospect is temporary or permanent migration. East Europeans do not represent a failed, but important, alternative; they represent failure by the standard norms.[12]

Gellner's insights into the collapse of communism shed new light on how to write and reflect on history in the age of the decline and fall of secular ideocracies. As for the political implications of his critical perspective, he extends it not only to throw new light on the failures of totalitarianism, but also to rethink what he terms 'the western *laissez-faire* illusion'. According to Gellner, totalitarianism cannot run an industrial society, but neither can pure *laissez-faire*.[13] This is why Gellner favours a sceptical social democracy instead.

Most importantly, Gellner touches upon a sensitive issue. An American, a Brit or a German does not need to say a word about his or her identity, as it speaks itself with a voice of economic and political power of a given country. Yet an Eastern or East-Central European, having introduced him/herself or having been identified as one, necessarily has to switch to a historical-cultural or, more frequently, a post-Cold War narrative telling a moving story of his or her country's belonging, albeit disrupted and arrested, to the West.

Therefore, Eastern Europeans often do not have any other option than to submit their life stories and personal details to a political or cultural history lesson about their respective country, which is offered to Western Europeans. This is why they usually do not introduce themselves as flesh-and-blood human beings; instead, they tell a story about their country and its heroic efforts to become a presence in, and part of, the West.

In doing so, they are bound to become part of their country's historical narrative or to criticize that country in harsh terms just to be able to examine their own self-worth and to present their person. The ambiguity of their country easily allows them to improvise an identity that is allegedly deeply rooted in history and linguistic-cultural paraphernalia, as if a story-teller would have no other quality in his or her soul than exotic otherness or ambivalent and unpredictable belonging to the Western world – or, more symptomatically, Western civilization. The ambivalence, ambiguity, uneasiness, volatility, versatility and unpredictability of their belonging make them put to work their ready-made identity stories and documented narratives.

The less known and the more ambiguous your country is, the longer your historical-cultural narrative becomes. You are supposed to have a strong, distinct, resilient, yet curious and exotic identity precisely because you do not belong here. The need for a strong and versatile identity springs from loosening or abandoning the sense of belonging. We allow and even encourage others to be as distant as possible when we deny them access to our ideas and politics and we want them to serve as facts or empirical evidence that would support our theories and blueprints for social and moral order.

This is to say that, for a more sophisticated milieu in the West, Eastern Europeans become communist or postcommunist story-tellers; in less fortunate circumstances, they serve merely as living proof of the increase of the purchasing power or social mobility of Eastern Europeans. This forced production of self-introductory and self-justificatory narrative, not to say colonization of memory and self-comprehension, is what happened to Eastern Europe on the mental map of the West in the era of liquid modernity. Things were quite different in the era of solid modernity, though.

As Larry Wolff plausibly argues, Eastern Europe emerged on the mental map of Enlightenment philosophers as a vast and largely imagined territory of chaos, ambiguity, ambivalence, backwardness and barbarity, as opposed to harmony, rationality, lucidity and civilization emanating from Paris, France and Europe in general.[14] This sort of mental map and a curious, yet hardly accidental, trajectory of Enlightenment consciousness led Voltaire as far as depicting Russian, Polish or Bulgarian aristocrats in his philosophical tales and plays (in *Candide*, Voltaire disguises Prussians as Bulgarians), although he never visited Russia or Poland. The *philosophes* imagined Russia and its provinces as a perfect experimental territory for trying out their political ideas and projects. Jean-Jacques Rousseau attempted to draft a constitution for Poland without ever visiting the country. Denis Diderot served to the Russian Empress Katherine the Great as her chief librarian and mentor of philosophy. Voltaire confined his service of this kind to mentoring the Prussian Emperor Frederick the Great.

Small wonder that the French writer Prosper Mérimée, in his horror story *Lokis* (1869), set in Lithuania, depicts a noble who is half-bear and half-man and who enjoys feasting on human flesh ('lokis' – or, more precisely, 'lokys' – is the Lithuanian for 'bear'). Incidentally, the Lithuanian noble bears the name of one of the former European commissioners, Algirdas Šemeta ('Szemiot' is the Polish for 'Šemeta' – or the other way around, if you prefer). The Irish writer Abraham 'Bram' Stoker wrote, in the beautiful English town of Whitby, the vampire tale *Dracula* (1897), whose main character, Count Dracula, comes from Transylvania – the name of this part of Romania sounds as odd and unfamiliar to the ears of a European as that of Lithuania.

If this is so, why should we wonder, then, at the American writer Jonathan Franzen's novel *The Corrections* (2001), in which Lithuania is depicted as a backward and devastated country; or at Thomas Harris's crime novel *Hannibal Rising* (2006), whose main character, Hannibal Lecter, MD, a psychiatrist and cannibalistic serial killer, was born in Lithuania? All these fictional stories and characters located in what appears to be – and yet is not exactly – Europe, or is yet another Europe, allow us to arrive at the conclusion that anything can happen in Eastern Europe.

With good reason, therefore, a good part of Giacomo Casanova's adventures, as his *Histoire de ma vie* (1794) vividly testifies, occur in Russia. Or recall Baron Munchausen's incredible stories, penned by Rudolf Erich Raspe in *The Surprising Adventures of Baron Munchausen* (or *Baron Münchhausen's Narrative of his Marvelous Travels*, 1785), which lead us, among other places, to Livonia – that is, the Baltic lands.

However, no reason exists nowadays to describe Eastern Europe as a territory of ambiguity and ambivalence. Western Europe has lost its belief in the solid and lasting foundations of its own social and moral order. On the other hand, Islam and Muslim countries are cast as the only territory of overt and covert threats, fear and loathing. An Eastern European, if s/he happens to be an intellectual, having become a poor cousin instead of a rival or enemy, is bound to choose between (1) parroting Western Right-wing

Islamophobic propaganda, or Left-wing tirades against the USA; or (2) examining her/his own life and taking a moral stand, opening up for, and sympathizing with, those who have succeeded her/his compatriots as cultural/civilizational curiosities, newly produced enemies or evil forces.

Indifference as cold as ice, rather than contempt or intense loathing, is characteristic of Western Europe's attitude to present-day Eastern and Central Europe. Another threat to Eastern/Central European intellectuals, in terms of their marginalization or socio-political and sociocultural miscasting, comes from their own countries, where the traditional roles of intellectuals as the personification of the conscience and as the principal driving force behind the nation-building process disappeared over the past twenty years, as if those roles vanished in the air leaving no trace.

Being unable to enjoy their life and work in truly prestigious academic institutions, as none exist or are identified and celebrated as such in their countries of incessant change and direction-free transformation, Eastern and Central European academics and intellectuals are forced to choose between shifting their roles towards the field of political power and prestige – becoming *Realpolitik* experts and advisers, or specialists in public relations and entertainment at home (trying to escape marginalization and poverty) – and temporary or permanent migration to North American or Western European academic towns and universities.

ZB   Indeed, nationalisms come in all sorts – as you rightly put it, 'from conservative and liberal to exclusionary and radical'. Though all of them can be plotted (or rather traced oscillating) along the same axis, stretching between the poles of human solidarity and all-stops-pulled war-to-exhaustion guided by the winner-takes-all canon. I'd place Giuseppe Mazzini at the first pole and Heinrich Gotthard von Treitschke at the other.

According to Treitschke's gospel, peoples (*Volken?*) come in two categories: the first, virile, macho, gutsy and forceful – and the second effeminate and, all-in-all, impotent. The first are destined to colonize the lands on which the second squat – those barbarian lands populated by weaklings incapable of partaking in monumental rivalry and doomed to submit to the needs and wishes of the strong. A Social Darwinist first and last, Treitschke perceives the world as a stage for callous and ruthless

racial competition aimed at survival of the fittest and the unfits'
extinction as the sole mode of inter-communal cohabitation.
Looking around his own nation's homestead, Treitschke acclaimed
and cheered the 'pitiless racial struggle' of Germans against Lithuanians, Poles and Old Prussians, and foresaw the 'magic' emanating
from 'eastern German soil' to be 'fertilised' by 'noble German
blood'.[15] He is also remembered for coining the phrase 'Die Juden
sind unser Unglück'[16] ('The Jews are our misfortune'), which was
to become the motto of Julius Streicher's bloodthirsty *Der Stürmer*.
With Wilhelm Marr and Karl Eugen Dühring, he pioneered the
concept of 'racial purity' of the nation, and those of ' "Blutvermis-
chung" und "Mischkultur" ' ('mixing of blood and/or of cultures')
as the principal subversive factors threatening national/racial
self-assertion.

If Treitschke epitomizes one extreme of the axis along which
the budding nationalisms of the nation-building era oscillated,
Mazzini – perhaps the first person to visualize and propose a
unified Europe as a family of free, self-determining yet peaceable
and good-natured, nations – personifies the other. In a jarring
opposition to Treitschke's savage, gory and lethal reveries, he visualized, endorsed and advocated an affectionate association of free
peoples based on the common civilization of Europe and bound
to spawn 'il banchetto delle Nazioni sorelle' ('a banquet of sisterly
nations'); he pictured nationalism engaged not in competition, but
in mutual support, cordial cooperation, and virtuous emulation
of the free peoples to build a new freedom – nationalism, in short,
as an uplifting and ennobling idea, as well as a humanizing and
civilizing practice of solidarity in action. 'National home' did not
signify for Mazzini a fortress bristling with bayonets or a bridge-
head for military conquests, but a place cut out and fenced off
from the world of cut-throat competition and bloody conflicts – a
workshop inside which to develop and learn the skills of mutual
understanding and assistance, and in which to practise humanity
and amiable, warm-hearted togetherness. Or, as Göran Rosenberg, acute and insightful analyst of contemporary sociocultural
trends, would express it, more than a century after Mazzini: a
'warm circle',[17] in which inter-human loyalties are 'not derived
from external social logic, or from any economic cost–benefit
analysis', not grudgingly accepted because they are found to 'stand
to reason' after a cold-headed calculation or under the pressure

of whatever currently passes for politically or socially 'correct' – but embraced unreflexively and matter-of-factly; 'naturally', so to speak. And as I put it when commenting on Rosenberg's concept of the 'warm circle',[18] this is exactly 'why frost-bitten people dream of that magic circle and would wish to cut that other, cold world to its size and measure. Inside the "warm circle" they won't have to prove anything, and whatever they do they may expect sympathy and help.' Those people dream of a habitat in which safety, self-assurance and self-confidence come of right instead of resulting from an unending, never conclusively won, uphill struggle for the right to human dignity, recognition and respect. Well, they tend to dream, investing their hopes of dream-fulfilment in the nation, recycled into a fully and truly 'inclusive' community; now they yearn for that fulfilment yet more passionately, living as we all are in a thoroughly deregulated, forcefully individualized society of loners frightened by the prospect of abandonment and exclusion.

Now to another topic you raise and discuss in depth: the wide, albeit ambiguous (one is inclined to say daubed or cacophonic, as well as meandering) panorama of the Russian–Western interface over its tsarist and Soviet past and Putin's contemporaneity. You trace diligently and record with laudable clarity the convolutions of the half-opening and half-closing of Russia to the West and the West to Russia. In the picture you so vividly painted, one of the prime actors in that historical drama seems to be, however, unduly kept out of the limelight: the Russian Jewish 'intelligentsia' – of whom Vladimir Jabotinsky is believed to opine that it fell 'madly, shamefully in love with Russian culture'. Madly enough, let me add, to draw Russia by the scruff of the neck (or rather to attempt to do so) out of its centuries-long backwater desolation – straight, and in one giant leap, from the *arrière-garde* to the *avant-garde* of European civilization and the civilized world. But shamefully? Did he have in mind the inestimable contribution to the Russian – and through it, the world's – culture, by the great creative thinkers like Levinas, Shestov, Lotman, Luria, Vygotski, Jakobson, Pasternak, Ehrenburg, Marshak, Brodsky or Mandelstam – some of whom you name – and the huge pleïade of prodigious scientists and highest-calibre writers and artists you had no space and time to list? But what I have in mind, however, is not so much the roll-call of distinguished names as the role of emancipated Jewry as a peculiar collectivity – and, in many respects, unique social and cultural phenomenon – though one by no means confined inside the borders of the Russian Empire.

Eric Hobsbawm dedicated to that phenomenon one of his last studies.[19] His conclusion was that 'Enlightenment made it possible for Jews to make the second major contribution to world civilization since their original invention of a tribal monotheism that gave universalist ideas to the founders of Christianity and Islam.' After two millennia of marginality and almost unexceptional isolation from the mainstream of history, of Jewish self-segregation aided and abetted by an imposed confinement, it was 'as though the lid had been removed from a pressure cooker of talents'. A 'tiny stream', as Hobsbawm put it, turned rapidly 'into a massive river'. That river, however, gushed from local streams and transformed native cultures. For Germany, Hobsbawm quotes Theodor Fontane's observation that 'ein wirkliches interesse für deutsche Literatur hat nur diese Karl Emil Franzos gegend' (loosely translated: 'a genuine interest in German literature can be found only in this Karl Emil Franzos's surroundings') – the milieu gathered and invigorated by a man just emerged from the ghetto. The story of German intellectual salons run by Jewish men – and particularly Jewish women – dedicated to the exposition and praise of the beauty of German arts and poetry and through it of the 'German Spirit', as well as to the articulation of their unique qualities, has been widely researched and described. For the multicultural lands of the Habsburg monarchy, the educated public consisted principally of Jews, and 'it was as culturally German "middle Europeans" that these emancipated Jews saw themselves'.[20] Not that the Gentile hosts saw them in the same way. Jewish emancipation combined glory with a tragedy.[21]

Already, in 1912, a certain Moritz Goldstein asked a worried question, whose validity and timeliness his Jewish intellectual readers stoutly refused to accept: 'Suddenly, Jews are to be found in all the positions from which they are not deliberately excluded, they have made the task of the Germans their own, German cultural life seems to pass increasingly into Jewish hands [...] We Jews are administering the spiritual property of a nation which denies our right and our ability to do so.'[22]

What occasionally rubbed salt into an already festering wound was arrogant Jewish attempts to out-master their chosen masters in their own mastery – particularly if such attempts were suspected of being successful.

The case of German Jews was perhaps unique in its eerie mixture of ludicrous tragedy and sinister grotesque, but the overall pattern of an incurable, aporetic ambivalence triggered by the Enlightenment-inspired emancipation was repeated all over Europe, with few if any exceptions. I believe that ambivalence gives its unique shape to the specifically modern variety of antisemitism. Following the shock of the Holocaust, that modern variety seemed to be laid in the grave – even though there are increasing signs of its possible resurrection, even if couched some-times in a different vocabulary and resorting to different argu-ments. It returns from its exile into the unconscious or its assumed grave whenever and wherever the ancient call 'Back to your tents!' is heard, or the process of nation-building is undertaken or resumed, including in Eastern Europe, in which (as you repeat after Kavolis) 'it is not only individuals but also nations that claim "inalienable rights", the latter with more assurance of the justice of the claim (since the individual, not the nation, can be accused, at least by individuals composing it, of selfishness)'.

Just one more comment: Hobsbawm, rightly, considers a modicum of tension between the realities of Jewish social place-ment and the target of their desired and pursued assimilation as going some way towards explaining the mystery of suddenly exploding – though anything but everlasting – Jewish creativity. Among the proofs for that supposition, he mentions the fact that, until 2004, not a single Nobel Prize was won by Israelis – 'while 2 or perhaps 3 were won by the modest (150,000) Lithuanian-Jewish population of South Africa'.

LD In your book *Wasted Lives* (2004), you wrote about human beings and their lives being rendered useless – made disposable by globalization. No one needs or misses them; and when they disap-pear, the statistics, including various economic and security indica-tors, take a turn for the better. For example, the emigration of nearly a million people from Lithuania in just two decades was followed by the news that the country saw a remarkable drop in the rates of both unemployment and crime.

These people weren't missed until somebody started talking about senescence on a grand scale – the prospect that Lithuania,

Latvia and Estonia might end up with the EU's proportionally largest segment of retirees (old-age pensioners) supported by emigrants and immigrants. Before this economic logic and argumentation were allowed into the discussion, fully one-third of the Lithuanian nation had been successfully pushed back to the very margins of our conscious public life. The turning of human beings into statistical units is one of the symptoms of modern barbarism and of the contemporary world's moral blindness. The same is true of demoting men and women into factors of production and calling them human resources. In all these cases, human individuality and the mystery of being in this world are negated by making them subject to the service of anonymous forces and systems, as exemplified by public opinion surveys, technocratic networks of marketing and politics, and the statistics justifying the operations of these forces and networks.

In Spain, in particular, young people became the focus of attention only quite recently, when, thanks to the *indignados* protests, the realization sank in that more than half of them had no jobs. In other words, over 50 per cent of the younger generation moved from a status of virtual non-existence, from a total absence in the public eye, into the bright limelight of public consciousness only when the fact hit home that these were indeed awful numbers. It wasn't the dashed hopes and lives, the loss of faith in the future of one's country and of Europe as a whole, that frightened the political class and scared the masters of public opinion – it was just the blank statistics themselves that caused the anxiety and brought on the shock.

I once asked the Russian writer Andrei Bitov to comment on the phenomenon of the superfluous human being in Russian literature. In a literary seminar that was taking place in Sweden's Visby, he was speaking about Alexander Pushkin, who not only used this concept but elucidated the phenomenon itself as well in his novel-in-verse, *Eugene Onegin* (1825). Be that as it may, prior to this work and Mikhail Lermontov's *A Hero of Our Time* (1840), the first to call attention to the superfluous human being in Russia was Alexander Herzen, who, immediately after the crushing of the Decembrist Revolt, realized that there were people in Russia who would never find a place in politics, or even society. They were in the wrong historical period and the wrong part of the world. Something or somebody made a mistake here: maybe it was God, or history perhaps, or was it fate? Perhaps they had to be sacrificed in the name of a brighter future, as in a Greek tragedy. Bitov told me, without any agitation, that everything might be simpler still: there are, to tell the truth, situations, epochs and societies in which human beings are just redundant.

It strikes me that our epoch, too, can do perfectly well without human beings. We just don't need each other for any social plenitude, for human fulfilment. *Pars pro toto* is enough. We need parts instead of the whole. During elections, we need some votes; in a situation requiring the lowering of production costs, we need cheap labour; in order to create a safe, trustworthy and business-friendly environment, we need what's called solidarity (in other words, renouncing protest and not defending one's rights, instead of choosing emigration or degradation). In some cases, an anonymous mass is precisely what fills the bill: it is intensely desired and eagerly sought after by vote-hunting politicians who, before every election day, remember emigrants as an indispensable part of their electorate while electronic voting (which Lithuania is about to adopt, but hasn't yet) is going on. In other cases, this mass is what politicians try to run away from because they understand perfectly well that the problems causing people to leave everything behind in their homeland and move abroad are not capable of being solved in economically weak countries no longer separated by borders from economically stronger ones.

Ratings are impossible without an anonymous mass of spectators and voters; that's why we love Big Mr Anonymous for as long as he legitimizes us with his faceless, soulless loyalty. We cannot do without this mass if we are politicians, television producers, stars or anyone else claiming the right to be publicly known with a recognizable face and name. But as soon as this mass stops legitimizing us and turns to us, not in gestures of recognition and thus to recreate us over and over again, but in demanding that we take notice of their individual names and faces as they step out of this anonymous mass and thereby take on personal features of human pain, drama and tragedy, then we begin to wish and wash this mass away. Why? It's because we almost instinctively realize that its problems – the problems of the individual souls making up this mass – are insoluble in a world in which everything they seek has been promised to them but without their having been told when and at what cost all this will be available to them. In their own country? At home? Why no, no way.

Where are the great promises of modernity to be found? Mobility, freedom of movement and the freedom of choice – weren't these promised to them? And wasn't one of the promises a world without borders as well? But such a world wouldn't be conducive to small, economically and politically infirm countries gaining strength. In such a world, powerful states would get stronger and weak ones would get weaker still. Wasn't it promised to us that we'd be able to cross any European border freely?

I'll put the situation in the words of a character in Marius Ivaškevičius's play *Expulsion* (2011), as staged by Oskaras Koršunovas. Eglė, the (anti)protagonist, says that crossing the border will be easy but there's one thing you'll have to leave behind, one thing you won't be able to take with you: your self-worth. When did this change happen: before the expulsion or after it? And what kind of expulsion are we talking about here? Is it a self-expulsion in the sense of *let's get out of here*? Or is it an expelling in the sense of *let's get rid of it* – a deliberate jettisoning of something that painfully testifies to your own or the system's faults? Moreover, will you be allowed to be yourself? Or will you have to transform yourself into a monkey, a pitiful socio-political parakeet parroting the accent, vocabulary, manners, tone, timbre and body movements of upper-class people?

The collective actor in the drama of expulsion is Big Mr Anonymous. When I use this name, I have in mind the whole anonymity-enabling system that consists of operators and those operated upon; of repressive organs and their victims trying to survive. The direct actors, who first of all possess nicknames and only then have first and last names, constitute our Lithuanian *precariat*. This is globalization's new lower class, in place of Karl Marx's proletariat: they are the precariously, unsafely situated people living in a zone of ever-present danger and risk. Nothing is guaranteed to them, they can't be certain about anything; their sense of security has been taken away from them forever.

Yes, they can attain some prosperity, but only through a kind of social suicide by becoming part of the great Nothing in a foreign country. This *precariat* embodies and serves the global network of anonymous persons and organizations, a network that starts with statistics and ends with a really existing variety that is held to be sufficient proof of the fact that society allows the impregnable existence of shocking social contrasts and inequalities. These will be liberally explained away by cultural differences and their right to exist with dignity and be as they are and be left alone, without having imposed on them sensitivities and interpretations that are foreign to them, or even being given any political or economic power. Thus you become part of the workforce, with the right to imitate the proper local accents and the consumption patterns of the jet-set classes, but without the right to your own authentic historical-political narrative and your own cultural ways of interpreting yourself.

East European self-contempt and self-hatred has deep roots, which in Russian culture are so profound that they can lead to a philosophy of history and culture well expressed in Pyotr Chaadayev's *Philosophical Letters* (1826–31), not to mention his contemporary Vladimir Pecherin, the nineteenth-century Russian poet and thinker, who wrote the memorable lines: 'How sweet it is to hate one's native land and avidly desire its ruin – and in its ruin to discern the dawn of universal rebirth.' This is worth calling attention to, for such a disdain for what one is, such self-hatred, is by no means to be found only in the nineteenth- and twentieth-century trajectory of Jewish identity, something that the German Jewish writer Theodor Lessing called 'jüdischer Selbsthass'. Nor is it characteristic just of Afro-Americans, whose own self-hatred in their childhood and teenage years has elicited myriad studies.

What then is *Expulsion* about? About the presence of pain and profundity in a criminal's personality? About the presence, in heroism and crime, of a transcendental remnant about which we will never know? About the fact that 'human waste products' and their 'lives not worth living' are just awful and ethically blinding labels, insensitive masks beneath which are hidden the real reasons causing young Eastern/Central Europeans to embark on mass-scale emigration that can no longer be considered normal by any reckoning? Or about the fact that vengeance is scarcely overlaid in us by a thin crust of civilization? Or that barbarism hides in vengeance but a no lesser barbarism parades under the cover of respect for justice and the law?

Is *Expulsion* about being expelled? About the power and attraction of exile which, like the medieval Pied Piper of Hamelin (in reality Satan himself in disguise), draws all the young people out of town, leaving behind only the oldsters? Or is *Expulsion* about the dilemmas of freedom, which it is dreadful to experience and which you have to pay for with your own security and homeland, but which give you the chance to find and speak your own language and to grow up without waiting for others – convinced of their superiority to you and your land – to explain your condition? *Expulsion* doesn't answer all these questions. It doesn't have to. That's not a task for an epic. Answers to them are provided by life, which it is worth living, but only when you challenge yourself ethically in that life. Maybe even by paying the price of expulsion.

Here, again, we find ourselves in the world of TINA. There is no alternative. Capitalism, which had long been presented in Soviet high school textbooks as the major menace to humankind, now seems more aggressive and dynamic in post-Soviet societies than in far more moderate, timid, egalitarian, social-democratic, welfare-state-orientated and post-capitalist Western European countries. Sweden, Finland and the rest of the Nordic countries, for instance, can only marvel at what they perceive as a sort of old-fashioned, historically recycled and ruthless capitalism of the Balts – or, to put it in more conventional terms, the libertarian economy of Estonia and other Baltic countries. The countries that used to symbolize to Soviet citizens the embodiment of 'wild capitalism' with its overt glorification of the winners and contempt for the losers now appear to them as astonishingly communitarian, warm and humane.

Indeed, they are pure and innocent in comparison with the 'first come, first served' or 'grab the booty' or 'catch as catch can' type of mentality that paradoxically, albeit logically, blends with a sort of Marxism turned upside-down. This extremely vulgar variety of economic determinism and materialism in Lithuania and other East-Central European countries barely surprises those who know quite well that the last thing one could expect to be named among priorities is the issue of culture. There is no alternative.

ZB 'No one needs or misses them', you say. Exactly. For the first time in remembered history, a large part of humanity – the poorest, the most deprived, stripped of prospects and hope of a dignified and worthy life and expropriated from the means of extricating themselves from their misery – are denied a 'social function', and thereby a place in society. For the first time, the poor are 'of no use', have no role to play.

In the Middle Ages the poor provided a handy – prolific and constantly within reach – occasion for good deeds: a God's gift to every Christian worried about salvation of their soul and reserving posthumous residence in Heaven. In modern capitalism, they were a 'reserve army of labour', and so in times when the power of a nation was measured by the number of men capable of enduring the chores and drudgery of the factory floor and battlefield were seen as a priceless asset; it 'stood to reason' to take care of keeping them in good shape – well fed, shod and sheltered, always ready be recalled into active service; the need for a welfare state, concerned precisely with securing this condition, was 'beyond left and right', just as is now the belief that lifting the impoverished and the indolent out of their hardship and anguish is a waste of taxpayers' money. Few of us are nowadays concerned with the salvation of our soul, while the vision of the impending division of society into industrial workers and their employers together with the demand for massive conscript armies have been long buried and for all practical intents and purposes forgotten. Unlike the 'lower classes' of the Middle Ages (and, for that matter, the 'unemployed': the very prefix 'un' in that word obliquely reconfirmed the condition of 'being employed' as a norm that has been violated), the 'redundant' of today can be therefore – and are – classified, purely and simply, as useless and good for nothing: strictly a liability, not a conceivable asset; an updated version of *lebensunwertes Leben*, slightly veneered-over with a concoction of verbal gimmicks to hide the explicit brutality of the Nazi original. As you say, 'when they disappear, the statistics, including various economic and security indicators, take a turn for the better'. But they, stubbornly and probably with a malice aforethought, refuse to disappear, however hard the guardians of law and order might strive to keep them out of sight. Even the stage of 'demoting men and women into factors of production and calling them human resources' has been left behind. Redundant people are the 'underclass' – living at other people's expense. By no figment of the imagination can parasites be visualized as a 'resource'.

Michael Burawoy, until recently the President of the International Sociological Society,[23] reminds us of and recounts, as well as retrospectively re-evaluates, Karl Polanyi's seminal argument about the counterfactuality of positing labour (alongside land and money) as a commodity, in the capitalist practice of its 'commodification' – though only to conclude that our current condition is already marked by the gathering-force tendency to 'ex-commodification':

> The process of excommodification – the expulsion of entities from the market, entities that were formerly commodities but no longer. Excommodification captures the expanded production of waste – the idea that there are lots of useful things that, to their detriment, are expelled from the market. In the face of excommodification, commodification can be a very attractive prospect.
>
> As Joan Robinson said long ago, if there is a condition worse than exploitation it is not being exploited. In many places, and increasingly all over the world, expanding reservoirs of surplus labor make it a privilege to be exploited.

In addition, Burawoy warns, the trajectory starting from commodification and leading to ex-commodification is currently extended from manual labour to its intellectual counterpart. Knowledge joins the family of quasi-values embracing originally (manual) labour, land and money on their road to de-commodification. But let me quote a fragment from the 'Evangelii Gaudium', the Apostolic Exhortation by Pope Francis –words that strike at the heart of our present predicament and its immediate prospects:

> Just as the commandment 'Thou shalt not kill' sets a clear limit in order to safeguard the value of human life, today we also have to say 'thou shalt not' to an economy of exclusion and inequality. Such an economy kills. How can it be that it is not a news item when an elderly homeless person dies of exposure, but it is news when the stock market loses two points? This is a case of exclusion. Can we continue to stand by when food is thrown away while people are starving? This is a case of inequality. Today everything comes under the laws of competition and the survival of the fittest, where the powerful feed upon the powerless. As a consequence, masses of people find themselves excluded and marginalized: without work, without possibilities, without any means of escape.[24]

Human beings are themselves considered consumer goods to be used and then discarded. We have created a 'throw-away' culture which is now spreading. It is no longer simply about exploitation and oppression, but something new. Exclusion ultimately has to do with what it means to be a part of the society in which we live; those excluded are no longer society's underside or its fringes or its disenfranchised – they are no longer even a part of it. The excluded are not the 'exploited' but the outcast, the 'leftovers'.

> While the earnings of a minority are growing exponentially, so too is the gap separating the majority from the prosperity enjoyed by those happy few. This imbalance is the result of ideologies which defend the absolute autonomy of the marketplace and financial speculation. Consequently, they reject the right of the states, charged with vigilance to the common good, to exercise any form of control. A new tyranny is thus born, invisible and often virtual, which unilaterally and relentlessly imposes its own laws and rules. Debt and the accumulation of interest also make it difficult for countries to realize the potential of their own economies and keep citizens from enjoying their real purchasing power. To all this we can add widespread corruption and self-serving tax evasion, which have taken on worldwide dimensions. The thirst for power and possessions knows no limits. In this system, which tends to devour everything which stands in the way of increased profits, whatever is fragile, like the environment, is defenceless before the interests of a deified market, which become the only rule.[25]

The roots of the liquid variety of evil you and I struggle to lay bare have been unravelled in the above quotation with an exquisite, seldom-encountered precision and clarity. And so were the essentials of the four-point strategy of counter-action: 'No to an economy of exclusion [...] No to the new idolatry of money [...] No to a financial system which rules rather than serves [...] No to the inequality which spawns violence.' Those four commandments from the Pope should, in my view, inform the followers of Burawoy's call to action: 'In a world where markets are presented as the solution to all problems, an ideological challenge to the supremacy of the market is a crucial preliminary to any effective countermovement.'

That reminder applies to the exile of young Lithuanians (temporary or eternal, no one – including themselves – can tell) whose story I've learned from your crisply and juicily narrated contents of the play *Expulsion*. But they are not the only humans for whom, as you put it, no place was to be found in their own country. There are millions – perhaps dozens or hundreds of millions – of humans like them, wandering around the planet between the non-places they try hard, all-too-often in vain, to domesticate and make their own. Lucky are those among them who escape refugee or asylum-seeker camps, those non-places with wide open entry gates yet tightly locked exits. For those lucky ones, however, nothing better is left in which to invest their hopes than life-rafts botched up cottage-industry-style.

4

Shadows of Forgotten Ancestors?
Manichaeism Revisited

Leonidas Donskis Like any propensity to think in polarities, portraying the world in black and white, the Manichaean divides have their charms. They find a way to penetrate modern philosophical theories and political doctrines, always leaving the same trace behind the message: there is no alternative. Love thy fate. This is the way in which modern fatalism and determinism make their appearance.

No matter how popular Oswald Spengler is expected to become once again, due to the profound crisis in Europe, one thing does not allow me to take him seriously. True, he made many subtle points as regards the decline of Europe between the two world wars, yet one of the most dubious ideas defended by the author of *Der Untergang des Abendlandes* (1918–22; *The Decline of the West*) was that of the parallel and separate existence of cultures.

For Spengler, even the slightest attempt to emulate, or at least to get closer to, the forms of another culture was nothing short of what he termed 'pseudomorphosis' – a false spread and interplay of cultural forms. The example that Spengler gave was a pseudomorphosis in Westernizing policies undertaken by Peter the Great in Russia. According to Spengler, the building of Saint Petersburg was nothing but a parallel reality in non-European Russia. This was exemplified by the reaction of Slavophiles who felt deeply hostile to Europe.

Yes, and no – that's how I would react to this. Whereas Russian politics had little if anything to do with modern Europe, Russian literature and culture were one of Europe's miracles. Even if Dostoevsky thought that nothing was as ephemeral and remote from Russian reality as Saint Petersburg, his own novels were bound to become part of the European cultural canon. Three examples that I would like to take can expose the Spenglerian fallacy better than anything else.

Firstly, let us recall an eminent film director, Sergei Parajanov (1924–90), who lived in the former Soviet Union, and who was a great example of the canon as a continuing rediscovery of the self in the world of multiple identities, and as a shared space of cultural identity. He was born into an Armenian family in Tbilisi, now Georgia, and spent much time in Ukraine and Georgia, finally settling in Armenia. All of these countries considered him to be one of their own. He spoke several languages. Incidentally, this was at a time when it was possible to play the ethnocultural identity card, precisely because the Soviets started allowing such minor identity games.

Parajanov went to Ukraine to make a magnificent film, *Shadows of Forgotten Ancestors* (1965), which is regarded as a classic in Ukraine, and the Ukrainians acknowledged the film as a significant part of their national rebirth movement. It is full of religious and folkloric themes and did not fit the social-realism criteria of Soviet cinema at the time. That was how a person created himself while acting in several cultures, all of which were involved in a dialogue that was intertwined, constant, and had multiple strands. Parajanov achieved international fame and professional credit after the triumph of his film *The Colour of the Pomegranates* (1968). The film was a biography of Sayat Nova (1712–95), the 'King of Song', a great poet of Armenian origin who lived in Georgia, and who wrote in Armenian, Georgian, Persian and Azerbaijani Turkish. The greatest folk singer-songwriter that ever lived in the Caucasus, Sayat Nova would be unthinkable without the context of several languages and cultures.

When somebody mentions Ukrainian cinema, I immediately find myself thinking about two major film directors – as distant from one another as two people of genius can be. The masters in question are Sergei Parajanov and Kira Muratova. Sergei Parajanov's aforementioned masterpiece, *Shadows of Forgotten*

Ancestors, based on a story by Mykhailo Kotsiubynsky which reveals and portrays the unique Ukrainian Hutsul culture, was nothing short of a *tour de force*, yet it was just one meaningful episode in Parajanov's work, which is otherwise more related to Armenian, Georgian and Azeri cultures. Kira Muratova appears to be a more specifically Ukrainian phenomenon.

Sergei Parajanov's at once timeless and novel cinematographic language signified the arrival of the new era of cinema in the eyes of such Italian masters as Vittorio De Sica, Federico Fellini and Marcello Mastroianni (Mastroianni and Parajanov, who held each other in admiration and the highest esteem, had once met in Tbilisi, Georgia). Yet Kira Muratova appears deeply grounded in modern Ukrainian society and culture, without which it would be difficult to decipher her complex cultural codes and allusions.

The world of Kira Muratova is deeply permeated with a special sort of feminism which would be impossible to find anywhere in the West. Western European feminism is about emancipation and liberation of women from social roles and frames of meaning imposed on them by the male world of power and symbolic authority; yet Eastern European feminism insists on female beauty, mystery and women's unquestionable superiority over the world shaped and orchestrated by men. In Western Europe, a feminist appears as a militant social and cultural critic; in Eastern Europe – as *une femme fatale*.

Mapping the world of Muratova's ethical and aesthetical sensitivities would be unthinkable without un-feminist feminism, a paradoxical thing which can only be explained by the inner nature of liberation for men and women in Eastern Europe. Freedom can never be ideological here, as ideology has always signified fraud and manipulation. In Western Europe, feminism could become a brother-in-arms to Marxism or any other sort of critical theory and resistance knowledge. In Eastern Europe, women either become beautiful and mysterious, or they run the risk of being reduced to that obscure object of desire – to recall Luis Buñuel's film *Cet obscur objet du désir* (1977).

Femininity, beauty, mystery, secrecy, and at least several planes of female identity (or trauma) are indispensable in Muratova's cinematographic world. Women are beautiful, sensitive, altruistic, caring (or monstrous as Ofelia/Ofa in *Three Stories*), yet they are never ordinary or forgettable. It is hardly accidental that her favourite actresses are cast in such a way as to bear family resemblance to the stars of silent cinematography. This applies to Muratova's actresses Alla Demidova and Nina Ruslanova, but it culminates with Renata Litvinova and Natalya Buzko, both inseparable from Muratova's world of mystery and femininity.

In addition, Muratova's world would be incomplete without grotesque figures – various kinds of crooks, charlatans, thieves and freaks, played by Georgi Deliyev (especially his unforgettable role in *Tuner*), Vladimir Komarov, Zhan Daniel, and a plethora of occasional actors. In this, Muratova closes ranks with Federico Fellini and Pier Paolo Pasolini, who relied on a non-professional cast. The blend of naïveté, spontaneity, melancholy, fun, laughter and the charms of unpredictable aspects of human life allow a point of entry into the world of magic – that sort of cinema unspoiled by literary narratives and clichés, popular culture or TV.

The Odessa connection cannot be misleading here, as Deliyev, Komarov and Buzko were all comedians from the legendary pantomime and clowning troupe Masks run by Deliyev himself. A carnival-like atmosphere, coupled with the sensation of the unreal, exposes Muratova's ideal of the film as a dream. Ingmar Bergman wrote, in his memoir *Laterna Magica* (1987), that to dwell in the space of a dream is an ambition of every true film director. Bergman was convinced that he himself achieved this only rarely, and that he fulfilled himself as an artist only in those infrequent moments when his films opened up into the world of dreams. Andrei Tarkovsky – whom Bergman always admired and held to be the greatest film director of their time – according to Bergman, remained unsurpassed as a master whose films became inseparable from the space of a dream.

So is Kira Muratova – an artist of the world of dreams *par excellence*. Mercutio's words from his monologue in William Shakespeare's *Romeo and Juliet* – 'True, I talk of dreams, / Which are the children of an idle brain, / Begot of nothing but vain fantasy' – would be the best motto for some of her films. The film as a continuation of a dream which we have once had and, ever since, were unable to forget, slowly recollecting an outline of the world around us – this is her only and true aesthetic reality. Muratova appears as a type of artist who never quite engages with reality as it is, as if to say that too much reality will kill us. Instead, we have to be prepared to save our dreams, unspoken truths, small parallel worlds and alternative reality, or our imagination, memory, and intimacy.

The stunning and penetrating beauty of Muratova's black-and-white aesthetics, accompanied by the magic touch of the great Ukrainian composer Valentin Silvestrov's music, manages to make up the aforementioned alternative reality – the one in which the forms of political madness, folly and hatred practised by the aggressively obedient moral majority retreat, disappear, and cede that to all of us.

Therefore, it is hardly possible to squeeze the cultural canon as it stands today in our modern world into a single culture. The ability to place something exclusively in one culture means that we have merely a political invention or a political project masquerading as culture. Instead, Europe is born each time that one culture gets permeated and rediscovered by another culture. Europe is not about purity; it is rather about the ability to live someone else's life in terms of a plot, narrative and memory.

Secondly, we could remember Sergei Parajanov's classmates in the VGIK (All-Union State Institute of Cinematography in Moscow), Aleksandr Alov and Vladimir Naumov, who had long worked together making several masterpieces, and who, perhaps, will best be remembered for their timeless films *Flight* (1970; based on the Mikhail Bulgakov novel *White Guard*) and *Legend of Tijl* (1970; based on Charles de Coster's *The Legend of the Glorious Adventures of Tijl Uilenspiegel in the Land of Flanders and Elsewhere*).

Legend of Tijl was nothing short of a triumph. The mystery of liberty deeply entrenched in the Flemish masterpiece was refracted through the profound drama of the Russian love for liberty – no matter how deeply abused and disappointed it was by the reality of the twentieth century. Coupled with great camera-work and with epic brushstrokes, this film revealed the stunning beauty of Flemish portraits and religious painting dating back to the Flemish Primitives. Actors' faces, eyes, hands and long gazes were straight from Rogier van der Weyden's or Hans Memling's portraits. The film had a double plane of aesthetic existence: whereas its longing for freedom and celebration of rebellion were too obvious to need emphasis, the film was permeated by a love of early modernity and of what could be described as an explosion of European culture which is so manifestly powerful in the early discovery of human individuality.

Thirdly, there was Emir Kusturica's first English-language film, *Arizona Dream* (1993), in which the otherness, if not the other-worldliness, of Southwest USA was revealed through the surrealist interplay of love, sex and death, which was best embodied in the profoundly European music of Goran Bregović as well as in a deeply Serbian view of the ambivalence of multiculturalism and otherness – something that the tragedy of Sarajevo alone can teach us.

Oswald Spengler had not seen all of this, alas. The shadows of the forgotten ancestors – who are they? They are all the incarna-tions of fatalistic beliefs in the infallibility of inevitable decline. In fact, here we hear the voice of the culture of determinism, as Vytautas Kavolis once christened this phenomenon, which he sug-gested was deeply rooted in a modern system of moralization. Kavolis puts it thus:

> A modern amoral culture, in the sense that it tends to eliminate the notion of individual moral responsibility without taking collective responsibility seriously, is the *culture of determinism*. In this culture it is assumed that individuals are shaped and moved by biological or social forces in all essentials beyond the control, or even the possibility of major choices, of individuals affected by them. The four major intellectual foci of this culture are the theory that 'biology (or racial inheritance) is destiny'; the belief that the human being is and should be nothing but a utility-calculating, pleasure-maximizing machine; the conviction that the individual is, in currently existing societies, only a victim of the 'oppressive', 'impoverished', 'devitalizing', or 'traditionally constricted' social conditions of his or her existence (without the ability to become an agent of his fate and assume responsibility for her actions); and the notion that he can be helped out of such conditions solely by the 'guidance of experts' who have a 'rational social policy' at their disposal, in the determination of which those who are to be helped participate merely as instruments of the experts.[1]

Kavolis's concept of a modern amoral culture sheds new light on why victimized groups or societies relate to the ruling elites as patients to diagnosing and curing specialists. At the same time, it allows us an essential comprehensive insight: we can understand why and how victimized culture manifests itself as the culture of destiny and determinism – in contrast to the culture of freedom and choice.

This concept reveals the links between all kinds of deterministic theories, especially in the social sciences. Kavolis starts by quoting Sigmund Freud's dictum, 'Biology is destiny', and then goes on to show other modes of discourse that speak out in favour of inexorable laws of racial inheritance, history, milieu, societal life, social organization and so forth. A modern amoral culture denying individual responsibility and moral choice – or the culture of determinism in Kavolis's terms – is a system of moralization disseminated in the modern moral imagination. Hence, we can identify what might be called natural innocence and victimization. According to this attitude, people cannot in principle control biological or social forces. On the contrary, particular individuals and even entire societies are shaped and moved by those forces. Since the world is controlled and dominated by powerful groups, clandestine international organizations or secret agencies and their elusive experts, individuals cannot assume moral responsibility for their actions. Nor can they influence or change the state of affairs. Such an attitude is characteristic of marginalized and victimized groups, but it is equally characteristic of the kind of consciousness shaped by anti-liberal and anti-democratic regimes.

In fact, racism in the nineteenth century manifested itself as a tragic anthropology and as a predecessor of the *Kulturpessimismus* of the twentieth century. Joseph Arthur de Gobineau may have been an early precursor of the tragic conservative consciousness of nineteenth- and twentieth-century Europe, along with Heinrich Rückert, Nikolai Davilevsky, Leo Frobenius, Oswald Spengler, Feliks Koneczny, Egon Friedell, Anton Hilckman, Pitirim A. Sorokin, Constantin Noica, Lucian Blaga, Othmar Anderle, Arnold J. Toynbee, and other theorists of the morphology of culture.

Was the morphology of culture a covert form of modern Manichaeism, this ancient belief in the parallel existence of Light and Darkness, or Good and Evil, which assumes that every form of withering and fading away is inexorable evil and destruction of life – which may well masquerade as the deterministic concept of science or as a poetic philosophy of culture? This question makes it worthwhile rereading and reinterpreting Voltaire's

Candide, ou l'optimisme, in which we find an existential and philosophical tension not only between the Leibnizean monadology and theodicy-centred naïveté of Dr Pangloss and the travel-and-experience-based wisdom of Candidè, but also between their modern (and nearly equally biased) assumptions and the ancient form of sombre wisdom of Martin the Manichaean.

Recall Czesław Miłosz 's confession, made in his interviews and also in his book of memoirs, *Miłosz 's ABC* (1997), that he had always regarded the theory of evolution as a theology of evil. Curiously enough, Charles Darwin himself believed that the survival of the fittest as a critical component of the theory of evolution smacked of a theology of evil in which the forms of life and death are deeply intertwined, interchangeable and, in effect, of no importance.

A striking aspect of Czesław Miłosz's worldview lies in his concept of evil, which seems manifestly Manichaean: like Mikhail Bulgakov and Simone Weil, Miłosz had never quite accepted the Christian/Augustinian or modern liberal concepts of evil, assuming that evil lives a life of its own and exposes a parallel reality. In fact, Miłosz 's self-confessed variety of modern Manichaeism, no matter whether we take it as an Eastern and Central European idiosyncrasy or as a deeply tragic and inevitable aspect of the totalitarian modernization of that part of Europe, calls for a separate and painstaking study.

Does it make any sense to attempt a philosophical interpretation of the world of TINA as a sort of applied determinism and also as a covert form of fatalism with some Manichaean nuances?

ZB You write of 'parallel and separate existence of cultures' which are, however, 'involved in a dialogue that was intertwined, constant, and had multiple strands'; of a person creating himself 'while acting in several cultures', but then also, quoting Kavolis, of 'individuals [being] shaped and moved by biological or social forces in all essentials beyond [their] control, or even the possibility of major choices'. Behind all such genuinely or putatively contradictory statements, stand the visions of a 'culture of determinism' confronting (let me use this phrase as the antonym) a 'culture of self-creation', in a war between implacably incompatible opposites – a war to the adversary's unconditional surrender. Let me deploy for a moment the war-cry of the age of totalitarianism, bequeathed to us by the shadows of our (un?) forgotten ancestors and languishing in the nooks and crannies of our (un?)conscious – the 'survival of the fittest' – in just this, protracted and probably unfinishable war of uncompromising and apparently unbendable visions.

It was actually Herbert Spencer, not Charles Darwin, who coined the phrase 'survival of the fittest' in his *Principles of Biology*, published in 1864. In Spencer's view, that phrase expressed crisply the essence of Darwin's idea of 'natural selection'. Darwin himself used that phrase only in the 1869 fifth edition of his *On the Origin of Species*. But did the two men have the same phenomenon in mind when using the same phrase? For Darwin, the fly-wheel of 'natural selection' was being better designed for an immediate local environment – whereas Spencer wrote of the preservation of favoured races in their life-and-death combat. Different approaches to a suspiciously pleonastic expression (Who survives? The fittest. But who are the fittest? Those who survive), and two sharply differing moral messages. Tautology or not, Darwin defines ability to survive by the fitness of the survivors (by which he means, let me repeat, better adaptation to the current/ local conditions), while Spencer reverses the order defining fitness by the fact of surviving others (outliving others being fitness's sole – both necessary and sufficient – proof). There is a straight line leading from Hobbes's *bellum omnium contra omnes*, through Spencer's survival of the fittest, to the more recent (1992–6) Samuel P. Huntington's 'clash of civilizations'. Following Darwin's idea, we may, however, ask what categories of attitudes and life strategies are better designed/adapted and suited for our current, timebound existential condition? In that case, we need to start by scrutinizing the features of the latter.

One feature which strikes me as most relevant to our issue is the fact of living in a multicultural world – a product of a massive migration of ideas, values and beliefs, as well as their human carriers. Physical separation, if still conceivable (a moot question), no longer assures spiritual distance. 'Their God' and 'ours' have their respective temples built in each other's immediate (fleshy, not just electronic) neighbourhood; inside the online universe in which we all spend an already considerable and still fast-swelling chunk of our waking time, all temples are located at the same distance – or, more to the point, in close space–time proximity. We should be careful, however, to set apart the two notions that are all-too-often misleadingly deployed interchangeably in the public vocabulary: multiculturality and multiculturalism. The first denotes realities (of surroundings, life-scene, ambiance); the second, an attitude, policy or life-strategy of choice. In his most recent oeuvre, one of the strongest Polish philosophers, Piotr Nowak,[2] subjects to a thorough vivisection the critique of the second of the pair – the multiculturalist attitude and/or programme – by Stanley Fish, the *enfant terrible* of the sedate establishment of scholarship.[3]

Fish distinguishes two varieties of multiculturalism: 'boutique' and 'strong'. The first is marked by the jarring contradiction endemic to the 'politically correct' incantation of principles – which (in Nowak's words) 'emphasize the importance of proper relations between coexisting cultures as well as the respect and sympathy allegedly bestowed upon them; on the other hand however [it] throttles rage and allergy aroused by the genuine disparities found vexing and offending'. And, dedicated as it insists on being to principles of tolerance, neutrality, impartiality, open-mindedness and fairness, and convinced (wrongly) of their universality, 'boutique multiculturalism' fails to comprehend others who treat their – however idiosyncratic and repellent – convictions and life routines seriously and cling to them really devotedly, rigidly and tightly. The second, strong version of multiculturalism goes, so to speak, the whole hog: it accords every culture an infrangible and indisputable right to practise whatever it considers right and proper, as well as barring all external critique of, let alone interference in, the practices this or that culture promotes. As Nowak comments, a 'strong' multiculturalist falls into a trap from which for her or him there is no escape: would s/he go as far as allowing cannibals to eat the meat they like most? But let us give voice to Fish himself in *The Trouble with Principle*:

> Boutique multiculturalism is the multiculturalism of ethnic restaurants, weekend festivals, and high-profile flirtations with the other in the manner satirized by Tom Wolfe under the rubric 'radical chic'. Boutique multiculturalism is characterized by its superficial or cosmetic relationship to the objects of its affection. Boutique multiculturalists admire or appreciate or enjoy or sympathize with or (at the very least) 'recognize the legitimacy of' the traditions of cultures other than their own; but boutique multiculturalists will always stop short of approving other cultures at a point where

some value at their center generates an act that offends against the canons of civilized decency as they have been either declared or assumed.[4]

The politics of difference [a term coined by Charles Taylor] is what I mean by strong multiculturalism. It is strong because it values difference in and for itself [...] Whereas the boutique multicultur-alist will accord a superficial respect to cultures other than his own – a respect that he will withdraw when he finds the practices of a culture irrational or inhumane – a strong multiculturalist will want to accord a *deep* respect to all cultures at their core, for he believes that each has the right to form its own identity and nourish its own sense of what is rational and humane. For the strong multicultural-ist, the first principle is not rationality [...] but tolerance.[5]

As Nowak sums this up, 'either a boutique multiculturalism, or none, as the strong multiculturalism is impossible – though its boutique alternative is but a pretence'. To conclude: multiculturality is reality, and a tough one, that can hardly be chased away or wished away. Differentiation of values and of the criteria for setting apart the proper from the improper, humane from inhuman and the decent from the indecent, as well as the awesome holding power of firm convictions and communal solidarities, are indeed facts of life. But 'multiculturalism', in its dual manifestation of a standpoint and a policy – both calculated to inform and trigger practices able to detoxify the unprepossessing consequences of that reality – sets a site for a tension-and-anxiety-ridden minefield rather than a (multi)theme amusement park. Coming to terms with migration, which in the absence of a viable policy of (and indeed willingness for) assimilation cannot but result in the pro-gressive diasporization of the life-scene, a skeleton key opening all doors or a panacea curing all the inner contradictions and cogni-tive dissonances such a life-scene is capable of (and prone to) generating is highly unlikely to be found. The art of peaceful, antagonism-free and mutually gratifying cohabitation is short on once-and-for-all valid rules and long on uncertainties, risks and frictions, as well as the need for improvisation. It also takes time – considerable time – to devise and learn such an art, with little hope of ever reaching the conclusion of the designing and learning effort that would render further swotting and sweating redundant.

If one needs one more of the numerous – I am tempted to say ubiquitous – illustrations of this aspect of our common predicament – namely of the failure of the liberal recipe for responding to its challenges – allow me to turn for a moment to Russia, a country whose historical meanders of fate and mood you watch much more closely and report much more expertly than I am capable of. Let me quote from Kirill Medvedev, in his youth a promising poet – though early disenchantment with literature and its narrow and self-enclosed world[6] forced him to change tack and immerse himself deeply in the role of public intellectual:

> The great intellectual mission of the 1990s was the creation of a new national ideology – either in its imperial version, when the centre, through the force of violence or through the force of its ideas (or, more likely, both), keeps together a host of different, and often hostile, political entities, or in its democratic version, where different entities come together on the basis of qualities and values they hold in common [...] the intelligentsia failed to do this. The political consequences are obvious – we were unable to form an ideology capable of creating a single living organism from various political and ethnic subjects living equally together. And the result was war – in Chechnya, in the streets of our towns and cities, and between the young and the old.[7]

As Medvedev observes, people under the emergent 'vulgar, vicious, largely ethnic-based clan capitalism', exposed to the new generation taught by 'the Komsomol activists [...] about contemporary values: careerism, success, drive, the "quick buck", etc.',[8] 'aggressively react to anything unfamiliar, not to mention anything that is actually alien [...] Right now radicals from both sides are fighting for the allegiance of precisely these people, and they're the ones who inspire fear in liberal centrists. In fact this fear is all that remains of the reasonable, judicious, "cultured" liberal intelligentsia'.[9]

Sounds familiar? It does to me. Excise a few local-folklore particulars, and what we read here is a report of the state of affairs in Europe and beyond.

LD In fact, several foci intersect and meet here: the culture of determinism is clearly only the tip of the iceberg when dealing with what might be termed the clash of the culture of choice and the culture of destiny, both deeply embedded in the mind-sets, the political and moral rhetorics and practices, of Eastern and Central European elites. It is hardly accidental that the intellectual and moral heroes of Eastern Europe in the late 1980s and the early 1990s were Karl R. Popper and his talented, though deeply unconventional, disciple George Soros: both were preaching the open society – the one with no monopoly on truth, and also devoid of any determinism-and-fatalism-ridden perception of reality. I would also add to this congregation of Eastern and Central European heroes of transformation the iconoclastic and sceptical gift of Ernest Gellner, and the profoundly democratic lessons of Ralf Dahrendorf drawn from the transformation and the new disenchantment of the world, in the Weberian sense, which Dahrendorf articulated in his epistolic dialogue with an imagined Polish gentleman, *Reflections on the Revolution in Europe*, modelled after the concept of Edmund Burke's classical – and profoundly conservative – reactions to the French Revolution.

Popper's polemical oeuvre *The Open Society and its Enemies* became a must-read in the 1980s, and quite understandably so. It was against everything we were taught to believe in: the idea that there must be a centre of gravity and a predictable logic in every segment of life; the idea of inexorable laws of history and social development; the conviction that great thinkers are all natural-born democrats and confessed liberals, almost by definition. Popper destroyed this set of clichés and naïve assumptions like a house of cards. Moreover, another study on the unquestionable value of the unpredictability and spontaneity of human life and societal existence, Popper's *The Poverty of Historicism* (1957), appeared as a direct confrontation with Karl Marx (exactly what was needed in the 1980s, one would think). Yet in addition to Marx, the gallery of thinkers dethroned by Popper included Oswald Spengler, Arnold J. Toynbee and other heroes of the cyclic interpretation of history and culture. In those days, we firmly believed that there *was* an alternative, there *should* and there *must* be one, no matter what was happening to us.

How ironic, then, that at the beginning of the twenty-first century, we find ourselves in the world of TINA disguised as a world of the rational-choice, profit-enhancing and pleasure-maximizing forces of the free market. Eastern and Central Europe – with a special role conferred on the Baltics – became the long and winding road from the TINA of Marxism–Leninism to the TINA of neoliberalism.

In fact, the world of TINA may come in many guises, ranging from economic and political determinism to the so-called 'morphological' interpretation of civilizations taken as mortal and finite islands of human creativity in the ocean of social and political forces beyond our control. Like Isaac Bashevis Singer, quite a few of them would gladly agree that causality is just a mask on the face of destiny. And Paul Valéry would serve here as a perfect example of how TINA originates from a poetic vision only to become a grim voice of fatalism and the self-contained logic of existence – as he was convinced that cultures are all mortal; and the First and the Second World Wars made a group of philosophers, from the aforementioned Oswald Spengler in his *Der Untergang des Abendlandes* to the Romanian philosopher and historian Neagu M. Djuvara in *Civilisations et lois historiques: essai d'étude comparée des civilisations*, translate this piece of poetic intuition into the language of a pessimistic and fatalistic philosophy of culture.

And here we have it. Overtly conflicting and mutually exclusive theories and approaches represented by evolutionists (whether we take Marx as one, along with Herbert Spencer, is a matter of debate, yet it is not without reason to view them in this way) and proponents of the cyclic view of history closed ranks, in the eyes of Popper and his followers, as friends to determinism and, subsequently, foes to spontaneity and unpredictability (which is tantamount to freedom in the European world of modern political and moral sensibilities). Whether we use 'progress' or 'development' or 'Untergang' or 'downfall' as a code word is of secondary importance. Like the myth of progress with all its promises to humanity and modernity, *Kulturpessimismus* and sombre interpretations of society, culture and civilization offered no way out from the predicaments of modern life. Prosper or perish, define or decline, beget or forget – yet the thing that would matter the least is your choice.

Here we are just a piece of fiction-writing away from a non-fictitious dilemma exposed by Aldous Huxley and George Orwell, and then reinterpreted by non-fiction authors such as Michel Foucault (the dilemma that you articulated so convincingly) – namely, the tyranny of happiness vis-à-vis the tyranny of hopelessness. Personally, I am, if truth be told, inclined to view the moral and political dilemma of the two aforementioned major dystopian writers as a fictional transposition of the conceptual alternative of the ideas of progress and decline in cyclic theories of history and culture.

This is why I would dare to reinterpret this paradigm as a modern variety of Manichaeism. There is something profoundly Manichaean in Yevgeny Zamyatin and George Orwell (and in Aldous Huxley as well, although to a far lesser extent), in terms of their belief in the indestructability of destruction and also in the parallel existence of evil. Probably, the narrator D-503 in Zamyatin's *We* is too weak a voice to speak on behalf of Light or Good, but his lover, a female dissenter, I-330, does qualify for the club of those who continue their hopeless fight for the remains of human decency and dignity. Much the same applies to Orwell's *1984* where a small piece of hope lies in the fragile and doomed relationship between Julia and Winston Smith.

How to define the Manichaean myth which seems so resilient in a modern world of pain, suffering, destruction and hopelessness (the world of Eastern Europe, to be more outspoken and precise)? Of the Manichaean myth, David J. Levy writes:

> But there is more to the Manichaean myth than the sum of the influences – Zoroastrian, Christian and Mesopotamian – that we can detect within it. There is a unity to the whole that gives it a grandeur and pathos all its own and allows us to speak, with Eliade, of the 'tragic pessimism' of the system. The source of this unity lies not in the diversity of historical origins to which the content of the myth bears witness. Rather, the myth illuminates, in a powerful way, the experience of the worldly evil and the aspiration to perfection of an imperfect form of life which is coeval with mankind. It is this, the existential rather than the historical root of the Manichaean world-view, which gives the myth its unity and even a certain outrageous plausibility.[10]

Do we have reason to regard the dystopia of the twentieth century (or the one of the twenty-first century, such as, for instance, *La possibilité d'une île* by Michel Houellebecq) as the novel of warning against the coming of the world of TINA? Or are dystopias themselves tinged, if not deeply permeated, by the original sin of fatalism and determinism? Are they against the world of TINA, or within it desperately trying to find the way out?

ZB   Mani composed the doctrine bearing his name in reaction to the (arguably) most acute and harrowing paradox, or rather anti-nomy, in the heart of Christianity – then the most dynamic and fast-spreading religious cult – and the resulting cognitive disso-nance: if God is, simultaneously, the epitome of goodness *and* omnipotent, how come there is so much evil in the world?! Either God is NOT love as the Christian scriptures insist, or He is NOT omnipotent as the Judeo-Christian dogma contends. The *Catholic Encyclopedia* admits that much, if not in so many words – without missing the opportunity to reassert the Church's pugnacious anti-Manichaean opposition:

> Manichæism professed to be a religion of pure reason as opposed to **Christian** credulity; it professed to explain the origin, the com-position, and the future of the **universe**; it had an answer for eve-rything and despised **Christianity**, which was full of mysteries. It was utterly unconscious that its every answer was a mystification or a whimsical invention; in fact, it gained mastery over men's minds by the astonishing completeness, minuteness, and consist-ency of its assertions.[11]

Indeed, Mani's doctrine 'gained mastery' over minds by capital-izing on their inborn yearning for logic and consistency, which the Christian antinomy defied; that doctrine owed its popularity (eventually dwarfed and smothered – though not by argument, but by an overt, violent and cruel, suppression) to the human, all-too-human passionate urge for non-contradiction, aided in addition, and abetted, by successive generations of teachers of philosophical wisdom. The *New World Encyclopaedia* is yet more explicit and resolute on this point:

> Manichaeism has a plausible explanation of the reason why evil as experienced in the world is substantial and virulent. As such, it compares favorably with the Augustinian Christian view that evil is non-being or non-substantial. However, its cosmic dualism of **God** and **Satan** is unacceptable to any monotheist who believes in one supreme God of goodness.

A key belief in Manichaeism is that there is no omnipotent good power. This claim addresses a theoretical part of the problem of evil by denying the infinite perfection of **God** and postulating the two equal and opposite powers mentioned previously. The human person is seen as a battleground for these powers: The good part is the **soul** (which is composed of light) and the bad part is the body (composed of dark **earth**). The soul defines the person and is incorruptible if there is complete abstinence, but it is under the domination of a foreign power.[12]

In short, Manichaean doctrine 'resolves' the antinomy and gets rid of the cognitive dissonance by separating – in space *and* time – God and Satan, embodiments respectively of Good and Evil: at the beginning of time, the kingdoms of God and Satan were held apart and their masters abstained, or were barred, from trespassing beyond the boundary – and that mutual distanciation will be restored in the course of time. The present incongruence is therefore a transient condition and a temporary irritant, brought into being by the invasion of the satanic forces; it is bound, however, to be overcome and left behind, and the clarity and transparency of the world and non-contradictoriness of human existence will be thereby restored, once the two kingdoms are again held strictly apart. That point was made particularly strongly in the *Encyclopaedia Britannica*:

> Whatever its details, the essential theme of this mythology remains constant: the soul is fallen, entangled with evil matter, and then liberated by the spirit or **nous**. The myth unfolds in three stages: a past period in which there was a separation of the two radically opposed substances – Spirit and Matter, Good and Evil, Light and Darkness; a middle period (corresponding to the present) during which the two substances are mixed; and a future period in which the original duality will be reestablished.[13]

To conquer, chase away and put paid to the offending contradiction, Mani resorted to rejecting one of the fundamental canons of Judaism and Christianity alike: the omnipotence of God. In Manichaeist teaching, God and Satan, Goodness and Evil, Light and Darkness are doomed to divide the universe between themselves – neither of the antagonists standing a chance of comprehensive and conclusive conquest of the other's territory. The dualism of powers burdens humans with inescapability of choice – but it also assures the plausibility of the choice's *Eindeutigkeit* (unambiguity). The task set by Mani for human participation in shaping of the universe's future is not the victory of goodness over evil, as this is beyond the realm of possibility – but finishing up their present-day (befuddling, confusing minds and adulterating actions) coexistence. I am inclined to suggest that the Manichaean equivalent of the Christian millennial vision of the Kingdom of God on Earth was the state of clarity and transparency, cleansed of the bane of ambiguity (and so also of all and any cognitive dissonances): for everything its place, and everything in its place – a condition putting paid to the torments of choosing, an end to the condition nagged and harrowed by the spectre/bane of an alternative. In the nutshell: TINA. TINA: in Freudian terms, the ultimate triumph of the 'is' over the 'becoming' – ultimately, of Thanatos over Libido. I am inclined to suspect that such a state of quietude, calm, composure, tranquillity, imperturbability (in short: ataraxia) has been and is bound to remain the unsung hero of *all* human millennial dreams in recorded utopian visions.

Nowadays, you say, 'we find ourselves in the world of TINA disguised as a world of the rational-choice, profit-enhancing and pleasure-maximizing forces of the free market'. You mention 'the long and winding road from the TINA of Marxism–Leninism to the TINA of neoliberalism'. And you rightly conclude: 'In fact, the world of TINA may come in many guises'. It may, and it does. I'd suggest that its life-expectancy is infinitely longer than that of any one of its successive incarnations; the TINA-world is capable of surviving the expiration of every one of them.

Human rebellion against the status quo, as well as the human desire to change it, were both more often than not prompted by the allure of perfection: of a state of affairs matching the definition composed once and for all at the threshold of the modern era by Leon Battista Alberti – namely, a condition in which any further change is both redundant and uncalled-for. In more down-to-earth terms, a place to disarm, unpack, settle and rest after the – as protracted as they have been exhausting – chores of travel. Or, in the nutshell, a condition with a beginning, albeit no end in time; a self-equilibrating condition, equipped with all the tools needed to secure its capability of returning to its 'normal' steady state after any conceivable distraction. All in all, a condition immune to all and any disturbance. A condition of the 'is' and the 'ought' merging and no longer distinguishable – let alone in conflict.

Please note that all utopias presaging or accompanying the birth of the modern era sketched the contours of TINA; and this proved to be, in my view, the prime cause of their downfall. Their fall from popularity ran parallel with the passage from the 'solid' (to wit, as was prompted to 'melt the solids' not by distaste for solidity, but because of diagnosing the extant solids as lacking in solidity) to the present-day 'liquid' (that is, melting solids out of resentment, revulsion and fear of all and any fixation) phase of the modern era. After the sombre and traumatizing experience of the two totalitarianisms' surge towards the end of history, those early modern utopias were re-baptized as 'totalitarian utopias' – tautologically as a matter of fact: that a mental excursion to a 'no alternative' condition, consisting in the suppression of all alternatives to itself – that common feature of the early modern utopias – has been now identified, as such, with a totalitarian bias and proclivity.

For better or worse, we have by now more or less settled in our permanently and incurably unstable and uncertain condition, experienced by many of us as felicitous, attractive and desirable (or at least, to paraphrase the memorable Winston Churchill's opinion of democracy, as the worst conceivable condition except for all the rest of them). For many of us – perhaps most – TINA moved from the family of utopias to the clan of dystopias. The perpetual rivalry between security and freedom (i.e., from 'more of the same' to 'the chance of a new start') for the pre-eminent location in the value hierarchy has, however, been anything but concluded – if the endemically entangled dialectics of those two cross-purpose, yet complementary, values renders a conclusion at all conceivable. Notorious excess, kaleidoscopic variety, inborn transience – indeed ephemerality – as well as the risk-pregnancy of alternatives may well resuscitate the fading charms of TINA (though this time in an opposite form to the Thatcherian–Reaganian rendition) – in the eyes of the classes downgraded and reduced by neoliberal realities to the status of a precariat.

'Some 8,000 helium balloons have been released into the night sky over Germany's capital at the culmination of events to mark the 25th anniversary of the fall of the Berlin Wall. Earlier,

Chancellor Angela Merkel said the fall of the wall had shown the world that dreams could come true' – so BBC radio informed its listeners on 9th November 2014. The progeny of those dreams, though, proved to be the thus far 25-year-long rule of the world deemed to allow no alternative to its neoliberal status quo. On that occasion, I published a brief essay on what 'living without alternative' means in practice in the Internet journal *Eutopia* – which I ended with the following conclusion: 'Twenty-five years ago people stormed a barbed-wired wall that embodied their un-freedom – hoping that once the walls are down, democracy will guarantee them freedom and freedom will assure their well-being. Twenty -five years after the wall fell, democracy is in a state of unprecedented (and then all but unimaginable) crisis.'

I can't resist the temptation to paraphrase slightly William Pitt Jr's statement, made in the House of Commons on 18 November 1783 – only substituting 'TINA' for the 'Necessity' in the original: 'TINA is the plea for every infringement of human freedom. It is argument of tyrants, it is the creed of slaves'. This applies to all varieties of TINA, whatever standard (including freedom in its neoliberal variety) it proclaims the absence of alternative to.

LD   Some authors are inclined to talk about the year 1989 as the autumn of the nations. There is something beautifully ambivalent in the concept of autumn – a Spengleresque motif of waning merges here with the metaphor of fertility and harvest: something straight out of the world of *Der Untergang des Abendlandes* by Oswald Spengler and *Herfsttij der Middeleeuwen* by Johan Huizinga.

The year 2014 marked the twenty-fifth anniversary of the fall of the Berlin Wall and of Eastern and Central European revolution in general. Even on cursory examination, 1989 appears to have been a year of significant upheaval. The Second World War with its sinister and seemingly insurmountable divisions within Europe ended nearly overnight, leaving no trace of the disbelief, despair and hopelessness that devastated Eastern and Central Europe for more than forty years. Instead, Europe was filled with joy and the sense of solidarity.

As Adam Michnik, a hero of the Solidarity movement and a towering figure among public intellectuals and dissenters in Central Europe, recently noticed, it is quite tempting nowadays to assume the role of having been the then-leading force and the major inspiration behind the historic fall of totalitarianism in Europe. Therefore, it was with sound reason that Michnik called the year 1989 the *annus mirabilis,* the miraculous year. In the United States, it is taken for granted that it was nothing other than the economic power of America that stripped the former Soviet Union of its potential, inflicting on it a humiliating defeat in the Cold War. German politicians would proudly assert that their wise and patient Ostpolitik was a decisive factor in this historic struggle, rather than the direct force and bellicose stance of America.

In Poland, nobody doubted that Pope John Paul II had come to delegitimize communism both as a world system and a major rival ideology, whereas the Solidarity movement dealt a fatal blow to the mortally wounded Soviet system, showing that the working-class people could revolt against the Working-Class State and deprive it of the remains of its legitimacy. In the Baltic States, it is widely assumed, and not without reason, that the living chain of the joined hands of Baltic people in 1989, which was followed by the exceptional role of Lithuania as the first rebellious and breakaway republic, also played a role in the disintegration of the Soviet Union and the collapse of communism in Europe – a role that was much too obvious to need emphasis. All these kinds of reasoning and arguments are more or less correct. If a unique combination of forces and inspirations had not been possible, 1989 would never have become the decisive year that changed history beyond recognition.

What looked for a Western European intellectual like the Grand March of History stretching from the Latin Quarter of Paris to the rest of the globe – as the character Franz from Milan Kundera's novel *The Unbearable Lightness of Being* (1984) has it – was a tragedy and the jackboot trampling on the face of a human being, in the way another character in the novel, Franz's mistress Sabina, a Czech artist in exile, describes it. Socialism and a promise of freedom as a theory in the West proved a horrible practice in the East in the year depicted by Kundera, 1968. Memory politics – as well as opposing memory regimes – still divides Europe. The short century of 1914–89 and the autumn of the nations were tragically logical in their overture, all their movements and their finale. Each time the world changed beyond recognition, there was a strong feeling of fatalism – a revolution, a war, a downfall, a criminal regime accompanied by complacency and the impotence of the so-called 'civilized' politics and institutions.

Words, words, words, and no explanations of what was lost, and why, or what kind of human and institutional weakness was fatal. We live in a time of obsession with a different sort of power. As you have pithily commented in your recent works, the old formula of politics as a carrots-and-sticks strategy still holds, yet we, having seen in the twentieth century the worst nightmares of sticks, are likely to fall prey to carrots nowadays. Power manifests itself as financial and economic might and potential, rather than military force and the language of militarism. Yet the logic remains the same. This is the good old *Wille zur Macht*, or the will-to-power, whether it assumes the guise of Friedrich Nietzsche or Karl Marx. The point is not whether you have an identifiable *Weltanschauung*, a resilient identity or a major ideology; instead, the point is about how much power you have. I buy, therefore, I am.

We have grown accustomed to regarding a human being merely as a statistical unit. It does not come as a shock to us to view human individuals as a workforce. The purchasing power of a society or the ability to consume became crucial criteria for evaluating the degree of suitability of a country to join the club of power, to which we apply the sonorous titles of various international organizations. The question of whether you are a democracy becomes relevant only when you have no power and therefore have to be controlled through the means of rhetorical or political sticks. If you are oil-rich or if you can consume or invest a great deal, it absolves you from your failure to respect modern political and moral sensibilities or to stay committed to civil liberties and human rights.

The crisis in the EU is quite different from all previous crises in the twentieth century. Before and after the Second World War, Europeans were afraid to name things that existed already; now, we are actively using words for things that have yet to come into existence. In fact, we live in a period of a fundamental interregnum. What is happening in present-day Europe is a silent technocratic revolution, rather than the rise of e-democracy and global civil society, as some of us choose to believe. A decade or two ago, it was crucial to have proof that you were a democracy to qualify for the club. What mattered was a set of values and commitments. But now, we are likely to enter a new stage in world politics: what really matters is your financial discipline, your ability to be suitable for fiscal union, and your economic conduct. There was a time when Eastern European nations sincerely believed that the rule of law, a strong commitment to democracy and a decent human rights record served as a passport to the heaven of Western attention, respect and even security.

Recalling Samuel Butler's *Erewhon* (the title of this anti-utopian novel is an anagram of *Nowhere* – hence, a clear allusion to Thomas More's *Utopia*), here we have the political and moral logic of Europe turned upside-down. In *Erewhon*, Butler pokes fun at a utopian community where illness has become a liability and where a failure to remain healthy and fit is prosecuted. Something of this kind can be found in Aldous Huxley's *Brave New World*, in which a failure to be happy is seen as a symptom of backwardness. A caricature of the pursuit of happiness in a distant technocratic and technological society should not reassure us that it is something beyond our reality, though.

What we have in Europe now is an emerging concept of the liability of economic impotence. No kind of political and economic impotence shall remain unpunished. This is to say that we no longer have a right to fail, which had long been an inescapable aspect of freedom. The right to be open to the possibility of bankruptcy or any other possibility of failure was part of the European saga of freedom as a fundamental choice we make every day, facing its consequences.

Those days are gone. Now you are at risk of becoming a gravedigger for Europe or even for the entire world if you send a wrong message to the global market. You may cause a global domino effect, thus letting down your foes and allies who depend equally on that same single-world power structure. This is a new language of power, hitherto unseen and unidentified by anybody in world history. Behave yourself, otherwise you will spoil the game and will let us down. In doing so, you will jeopardize the viability of a moral and social order within which no country or nation remains responsible for itself. Everything has its global repercussions and implications.

And what about nations? Up to now we were certain that the European nations embodied the Calvinist principle that predestination implies a possibility of being happy in this earthly life and in this worldly reality; the Kantian principle of self-determination was more relevant in the nineteenth century. There was a world where the pursuit of happiness, like the possibility of salvation and self-fulfilment, spoke the language of the republic and its values – hence, the emergence of postcolonial nations after two world wars and after the break-up of empires.

What we have today in our second modernity bears little, if any, resemblance to this logic of the first modernity, as Ulrich Beck would have it; we can no longer experience the passions and longings of the twentieth century, not to mention the dramas of the nineteenth century, no matter how hard we try to relegitimize our historical and political narrative. To use your terms, Zygmunt, liquid modernity transformed us into a global community of consumers. What was a nation in the era of solid modernity, as a community of memory, collective sentiment and moral choice, now is a community of consumers who are obliged and expected to behave in order to qualify for the club.

In the age of Facebook, nations are becoming extraterritorial units with a shared language and culture. We knew in the era of solid modernity that the nation was made up by several factors – first and foremost by a common territory, language and culture, as well as by the modern division of labour, social mobility and literacy. Nowadays, the picture is rather different: a nation appears as an ensemble of mobile individuals with their logic of life deeply embedded in withdrawal-and-return. It is a question of whether you are online or offline with regard to your country's problems and the debates around them, instead of deciding once and for all whether you are going to stay in that same place or vote for those same political actors for the rest of your days. Either you are on or you are off. This is the daily plebiscite of a liquid-modern society.

Arnold J. Toynbee, echoing a great many historians, once asked: does history repeat itself? Karl Marx wittily and caustically answered this question in the nineteenth century, reminding us that it does, and even twice: once as a tragedy and then as a farce. There are quite a few indications that what proved a Shakespearean tragedy in the twentieth century is tending to repeat itself as a farce now. The Soviet Union and its new industrial faith, as Ernest Gellner described it, was nothing short of a civilizational alternative and rival to Europe – or to the West, if you prefer. A deep disappointment with the supposed Jerusalem of the Left, along with the real collapse of modern belief (or disbelief) in a hidden alternative to capitalism and liberalism, had the components of a universal tragedy.

Yet what appears as the present-day civilizational rival to Europe is Russia's crony capitalism coupled with a gangster state, instead of a resistance ideology or a utopian dream. What was a tragic cul-de-sac of humanity turned into a grotesquery of a rogue state with a semi-criminal elite. Ideology without any ideology, or capitalism without liberty – no theory or ideological doctrine of the twentieth century can explain this phenomenon. Living in a post-ideological – and, in all likelihood, post-political – era creates quite a few predicaments when trying to apply the mainstream views or conventional wisdom of the past.

History does repeat itself – we will know soon as to whether it is doing so this time as a tragedy or as a farce. We will learn whether the new Iron Curtain and the Old New Cold War is about the impotence and forthcoming final disintegration of Russia or whether it is all about our own impotence, along with the crushing of our hopes of achieving the final breakthrough.

ZB All those people, individual and collective, named and anonymous, whom you listed as playing a part in the miracle of 1989, indeed contributed to the end of the communist empire and to the opening of a new chapter in European and planetary history. Your list is, however, incomplete. The most conspicuous among the absentees is, obviously, Mikhail Gorbachev. It would be tremendously difficult – nay, impossible, and indeed insane – to imagine the tide of 'velvet revolutions' – not just un-dammed, but by design as much as by default bolstered and boosted by the officially declared Kremlin non-intervention – toppling and drowning the 'system' if the spectre of the Brezhnev Doctrine had still hovered over the communist camp.

Perhaps less conspicuous – given the most common narratives of the *annus mirabilis*, such as Thomas Carlyle's *On Heroes, Hero-Worship, and the Heroic in History* – is the principal absentee: arguably the *sine qua non* hero of the end of the communist-system drama, the true *éminence grise* of the plot – *the system itself*. Made to the measure of the nineteenth-century experiences, projections and expectations of the solid-modern society of producers, it was singularly unfit to deal with the late twentieth-century realities of the liquid-modern society of consumers and their challenges. It could perhaps have gone on for a considerable time, still competing with its capitalist adversaries in chasing after ever higher figures for its mined-coal-and-smelted-iron statistics, were it not for its contestants opting out of the chase and switching to completely different yardsticks with which to measure, and entirely different indices with which to record and compare the aptitude and dexterity of socio-political systems. Let's recall Darwin's insistence, that natural selection favours the species 'better designed for an immediate local environment'. Well, the 'local environment' had changed beyond recognition since the time in which the design for the communist system was set; that change caught the system utterly unprepared and incapable of adjusting, let alone adapting. For a similar reason, as paleontologists teach us, mighty dinosaurs were once swept off the face of the earth.

Almost to the very end of the communist saga, the learned and highly esteemed luminaries of 'Sovietology' or 'Kremlinology' – a branch of scholarship the most lavishly provided for in the history of modern political sciences and awash with an unlimited supply of money – predicted but two possible scenarios for the planet split into two camps: MAD ('mutually assured destruction') or convergence (both sides learning/compromising to land somewhere in the middle). No one predicted what was in fact going to happen: that the communist system would implode instead of exploding, and collapse under the weight of its unfulfilled and in fact impossible-to-fulfil promises. The list of demands put to the Polish communist state by rebellious Solidarity was a roll-call of the communist state's broken oaths and unfulfilled pledges.

Well, a quarter of a century after that collapse, we have been ushered (to use the American folkloristic idiom) into an 'entirely different ball game'. You, as always correctly, sum that difference up in saying that nowadays, unlike before, 'power manifests itself as financial and economic might and potential, rather than military force and the language of militarism. Yet the logic remains the same.' Well, as popular wisdom has it, he who pays the piper sets the tune. In his farewell address of 1961, recorded as the 'Industrial–Military Complex speech', President Dwight Eisenhower reminded Americans that 'three and a half million men and women are directly engaged in the defense establishment. We annually spend on military security more than the net income of all United States corporations.' And he warned them, and exhorted:

> This conjunction of an immense military establishment and a large arms industry is new in the American experience. The total influence – economic, political, even spiritual – is felt in every city, every State house, every office of the Federal government. We recognize the imperative need for this development. Yet we must not fail to comprehend its grave implications. Our toil, resources and livelihood are all involved; so is the very structure of our society.[14]

Another 'complex', this time financial–consumerist, demands that 'we must not fail to comprehend its grave implications', memorious that 'the very structure of our society', 'our toil, resources and livelihood, all hang on it'. But, as you propose and I countersign, 'the logic remains the same'!

You invoke Samuel Butler's and Aldous Huxley's portents/premonitions to grasp the essence of life under the rule of the new complex – the tune set by the piper's new paymaster. But a long time before either of them reached for their pens, the great François Rabelais sketched the contours of things to come when he inscribed the following motto on the 'great gate' of l'Abbaye Thélème erected by his hero Gargantua:

> Gold give us, God forgive us,
> And from all woes relieve us;
> That we the treasure
> May reap of pleasure,
> And shun whate'er is grievous,
> Gold give us, God forgive us.[15]

Reaping the pleasures was one commandment that couldn't and wouldn't be disobeyed by the inmates of Thélème. In the words of Rabelais, 'in all their rule and strictest tie of their order there was but this one clause to be observed, DO WHAT THOU WILT'. Curiously though, that obligatory 'willing' proved to be in practice contagious – resulting in an endless succession of brief, scattered and spaced-out, but all the same all-affecting, epidemics:

> By this liberty they entered into a very laudable emulation to do all of them what they saw did please one. If any of the gallants or

ladies should say, Let us drink, they would all drink. If any one of them said, Let us play, they all played. If one said, Let us go a-walking into the fields they went all.[16]

Well, as you say and as I keep repeating after you, 'the logic remains the same': the logic of a remotely controlled swarm – in our reincarnation of Thélème, as much as in the original, a swarm of consumers.

In 1973, Jürgen Habermas argued in his *Legitimation Crisis* that the state is capitalist in as far as it assures regular and successful encounters between capital and labour, ending in a buying/selling transaction; in order to perform that function, the state needs to ensure that capital can afford to pay the price of labour, whilst labour is in a good enough state to entice its prospective buyers. The state ensures this by obliquely subsidizing capital through shifting onto taxpayers the costs of the health service, education, housing, etc., needed to keep the 'reserve army of labour' fit to be called into active service. Today the role of the state in sustaining the capitalist economy consists in assuring a regular and successful encounter between client and commodity. To perform that role, the state must obliquely subsidize the banking network and its stockholders through shifting onto taxpayers the risks involved in credit transactions, according to the rule of privatizing the gains and nationalizing the losses.

Visor up, all disguises thrown off. No mincing matters. As you say, 'what really matters is your financial discipline, your ability to be suitable for fiscal union, and your economic conduct'. There's no doubt who the master is, and how he selects – with a carrot or a stick, by enticement or conscription – the pipers to play his tunes. 'No kind of political and economic impotence shall remain unpunished' – is this correct, as you suggest? I'd rather say that no kind of political incompetence in forcing the tune to be played obediently, note after note as the score enjoins and commands, will remain unpunished. Insubordination won't be tolerated. If democracy does not guarantee subordination – that is, a policy of austerity, cuts in public spending, unbridling of labour markets and bridling of labour's defences and the like, though also of enforcement of credit-dependence – all the worse for democracy. It's all about the economy, stupid! Politics is about a rising Gross

Domestic Product, and the rise in the Gross Domestic Product is about the rich getting richer and the poor poorer.

However hawk-eyed one might be, it is horribly difficult to espy and detect a new Jerusalem on the Right or Left – or, indeed, in the centre. As 100 years ago, well before the start of the Left vs Right, catch-as-catch-can match, people keep, however, week-in week-out, repeating after William Blake:

> I will not cease from Mental Fight,
> Nor shall my Sword sleep in my hand:
> Till we have built Jerusalem,
> In England's green & pleasant Land.

As long as we follow that verse, we manage to keep TINA at a safe distance from our not-so-green and not-so-pleasant lands.

LD I would immediately reciprocate and close this chapter by recalling another piece by William Blake written with the stroke of genius – namely, his little poem 'The Fly', which I would describe as a profoundly anti-TINA poem:

> Little Fly,
> Thy summer's play
> My thoughtless hand
> Has brushed away.
>
> Am not I
> A fly like thee?
> Or art not thou
> A man like me?
>
> For I dance
> And drink, and sing,
> Till some blind hand
> Shall brush my wing.
>
> If thought is life
> And strength and breath
> And the want
> Of thought is death;
>
> Then am I
> A happy fly,
> If I live,
> Or if I die.[17]

What is a pessimist? A well-informed optimist, say the wags. Or an intelligent optimist, as many would reply. Today, few doubt that optimists, at best, are thought of as shallow and vapid and, to be even more frank, foolish and unwise. Somehow, it seems that to us profundity and wisdom are to be found in pessimism and apocalyptic prophecies. Horrifying accounts of the things that await us at the end of times have become a veritable cottage industry of fear (fear is second only to exposure in the list of most valuable commodities in politics and media); these are linked to questions of responsibility, seriousness and profundity, while optimism is akin to the grin of the village idiot, who rejoices because the sun's rays are golden and tomatoes are red.

In truth, the roots of this prejudice lie far deeper. The real problem is that we live in a world without alternatives. This world solemnly announces itself to be the only reality, taking as lunatics or at best eccentrics all those who believe that everything has an alternative, including even the very best models of governance and the most profound ideas (not to mention business and engineering projects). The world has probably never been so inundated with fatalistic and deterministic beliefs as it is today; alongside serious analyses, as if from a horn of plenty, flow prophecies and projections of looming crises, dangers, downward spirals and the end of the world. In this widespread atmosphere of fear and fatalism, the conviction arises that there are no alternatives to contemporary political logic and the tyranny of the economy, or to attitudes to science and technology and the relationship between nature and humanity.

Optimism is in no way a crass assumption that everything is wonderful – it is the view that evil is only a passing thing that is not capable of permanently destroying our humanity, and the conviction that there are always alternatives. Whatever the case, optimism flows not from naïveté or shallowness of thought but from great wisdom and experience; it is the faith that the world is always something incomparably greater than me and my surroundings, and is similar to me. If so, the mere fact of my being in the world and the possibility for thought and doubt is a gift deserving gratitude and appreciation, because everything could be – or could have been – far worse. I could quite simply not have *been*, which is why the question of my happiness and satisfaction is secondary. That I *am* in this world, and that I can reflect upon my place in it, bears witness to the fact that this world is the best of all possible worlds – because I do not exist in other worlds, it is up to someone else to resolve their goodness or badness.

Optimism can be not only historical but also metaphysical, anti-fatalistic, anti-deterministic. This kind of optimism was best expressed by Dylan Thomas in his timeless poem 'And Death Shall Have No Dominion' – a truly anti-TINA requiem for the twentieth century, a message to humanity more important now than ever before.

Notes

Introduction: On Liquid Evil and TINA

1 Vytautas Kavolis, 'Moral Cultures and Moral Logics', *Sociological Analysis* 38 (1977): 331–44; 'Civilizational Models of Evil' in M. Coleman Nelson and M. Eigen (eds.), *Evil: Self and Culture*, Human Sciences Press 1984, pp. 17–35; 'Logics of Evil as Secular Moralities', *Soundings* 68 (1985): 189–211; *Moralizing Cultures*, University Press of America 1993.

2 Zygmunt Bauman, *Consuming Life*, Polity, 2007; Zygmunt Bauman and Leonidas Donskis, *Moral Blindness: The Loss of Sensitivity in Liquid Modernity*, Polity 2013.

3 S. E. Igo, 'The Beginnings of the End of Privacy', *The Hedgehog Review* 17 (1) (Spring 2015): 18–29, p. 18.

4 Ibid., 28.

5 Ivan Krastev in *Journal of Democracy*, 25 (4) (October 2014).

6 Paul Auster and J. M. Coetzee, *Here and Now: Letters 2008–2011*, Vintage Books 2014, pp. 136 and 139.

7 Michel Serres, *Thumbelina: The Culture and Technology of Millennials*, trans. Daniel W. Smith, Rowman & Littlefield 2015, p. 5.

8 Ibid., p. 62.

9 Zygmunt Bauman, *Liquid Modernity*, Polity 2000.

1: From a Person to a Nonperson? Mapping Guilt, Adiaphora, Precariousness and Austerity

1 K. Jaspers, *Die Schuldfrage*, Artemis-Verlag 1947.

2 See P. Bruckner, *The Tyranny of Guilt: An Essay on Western Masochism*, Princeton University Press 2010.

3 Vytautas Kavolis, 'Moral Cultures and Moral Logics', *Sociological Analysis* 38 (1977): 331–44; 'Civilizational Models of Evil' in M. Coleman Nelson and M. Eigen (eds.), *Evil: Self and Culture*, Human Sciences Press 1984, pp. 17–35; 'Logics of Evil as Secular Moralities', *Soundings* 68 (1985): 189–211; *Moralizing Cultures*, University Press of America 1993.

4 Cited in T. Cushman, 'George Orwell: Ethnographer of Modernity', *The Hedgehog Review*, 15 (1) (2013): 69–77, p. 75.

5 Zygmunt Bauman and Leonidas Donskis, *Moral Blindness*, Polity 2013.

6 M. Gessen, 'The Weird and Instructive Story of Eduard Limonov', *The New York Review of Books*, 62 (9) (21 May – 3 June 2015): 45–7, p. 47.

7 Ibid.

8 See Immanuel Kant, 'Idea of a Universal History from a Cosmopolitan Point of View' [1784] in *Theories of History*, ed. Patrick Gardiner, Free Press 1959, pp. 22–34.

9 In *O Caderno*, here quoted from the English edition *The Notebook*, trans. Amanda Hopkinson and Daniel Hahn, Verso 2010, p. 29.

10 Jean-Claude Michéa in *L'empire du moindre mal*, Flammarion 2007; here quoted after David Fernbach's translation, *The Realm of Lesser Evil*, Polity 2009, p. 138.

11 Ibid., p. 139.

12 See Victor Turner, *The Ritual Process: Structure and Anti-Structure*, Aldine Transaction Press 2008.

13 Luke Dormehl, *The Formula: How Algorithms Solve All Our Problems…and Create More*, W. H. Allen 2014, p. 3.

14 As estimated by Barbara A. West, *Encyclopedia of the Peoples of Asia and Oceania*, Infobase Publishing 2008, p. 684.

15 Arne Johan Vetlesen, *Denial of Nature: Environmental Philosophy in the Era of Global Capitalism*, Routledge 2015, p. 2.

16 Ibid., pp. 16–17, citing Naomi Klein, *This Changes Everything: Capitalism vs. the Climate*, Allen Lane 2014, p. 169.

17 Vetlesen, *Denial of Nature*, p. 41, citing Teresa Brennan, *Exhausting Modernity: Grounds for a New Economy*, Routledge 2000, p. 131.

18 See, in particular, Lewis Mumford, *The City in History*, Harcourt, Brace & World 1961.

19 Ibid., pp. 450–1.

20 See Heidegger's 'The Question Concerning Technology' (1950), here quoted after http://simondon.ocular-witness.com/wp-content/uploads/2008/05/question_concerning_technology.pdf.

21 For more on this, see Leonidas Donskis (2009), *Troubled Identity and the Modern World*, Palgrave Macmillan 2009.

22 See Ken Jowitt, *New World Disorder: The Leninist Extinction*, University of California Press 1993.
23 Jeffrey Sommers and Charles Woolfson (eds.), *The Contradictions of Austerity: The Socio-Economic Costs of the Neoliberal Baltic Model*, Routledge 2014, p. xv.
24 Ibid., p. 139.
25 Ibid., p. xv.
26 Ibid., pp. 149–73, p. 150.
27 Ibid., p. xv.
28 Ibid., p. 64.
29 Ibid., p. 46.
30 Ibid., p. 3.
31 Ibid., p. xvi.
32 Ibid., p. 107.
33 Ibid., p. xvii.
34 In Carl Cederström and André Spicer, *The Wellness Syndrome*, Polity 2015, p. 1.
35 Ibid., pp. 3–4.
36 http://learn.fi.edu/learn/heart/vessels/capillaries.html.
37 www.medicinenet.com/script/main/art.asp?articlekey=2622.
38 http://nihseniorhealth.gov/leukemia/symptomsanddiagnosis/01.html.
39 Alenka Zupančič, *The Odd One In*, MIT Press 2008, p. 5.
40 Isabell Lorey in *State of Insecurity: Government of the Precarious*, Verso 2015, p. 2.
41 Ibid., p.64.
42 Ivor Southwood, *Non-Stop Inertia*, Zero Books 2011, p. 3.
43 Ibid., p. 37.

2: From the Kafkaesque to the Orwellesque?
War Is Peace, and Peace Is War

1 Personal message from Alena Ledeneva. See also www.russia-direct.org/qa/russia-you-cant-beat-sistema.
2 See Anna Wolff-Powęska, 'I ruszył kwiat młodzieży z narzędziami mordu' ('And the Bloom of Youth Took Off Carrying Tools of Murder'), *Gazeta Wyborcza*, 27 June 2014.
3 Hannah Arendt, *The Origins of Totalitarianism*, André Deutsch 1986, pp. 328ff.
4 Ibid., p. 334.
5 Ivan Krastev in *Journal of Democracy* 25 (4) (October 2014).
6 Michel Houellebecq and Bernard-Henri Lévy, *Public Enemies*, Atlantic Books 2011, p. 68.

7 See Timothy Snyder, 'Gogol Haunts the New Ukraine', *The New York Review of Books*, 57 (5) (25 March – 7 April 2010): 35–6, p. 35.
8 See Timothy Snyder, 'To Understand Putin, Read Orwell: Ukraine, Russia and the Big Lie', *POLITICO Magazine* (3 September 2014): www.politico.com/magazine/story/2014/09/to-understand-putin -read-orwell-110551.html#.VXrHcvmqqko.
9 Jean Baudrillard, *Simulacra and Simulation*, 1981.
10 See T. Cushman, 'George Orwell: Ethnographer of Modernity', *The Hedgehog Review*, 15 (1) (2013): 69–77.
11 Ibid., 74.
12 Krastev, *Journal of Democracy* 25 (4) (October 2014).
13 Trans. Tania Stern and James Stern in *The Collected Short Stories of Franz Kafka*, ed. Nahum N. Glatzer, Periguin 1988, p. 449.
14 Trans. Willa Muir and Edwin Muir in *The Collected Short Stories of Franz Kafka*, ed. Glatzer, p. 415.

3: Where Are the Great Promises of Modernity to Be Found? Fear and Loathing in the Brave New World

1 Milan Kundera, 'The Tragedy of Central Europe', trans. Edmund White, *The New York Review of Books*, 31 (7) (26 April 1984): 33–8.
2 Mark Lilla, 'Slouching Toward Mecca', *The New York Review of Books*, 62 (6) (2–22 April 2015): 41–3.
3 Yosef Hayim Yerushalmi, *Zakhor: Jewish History and Jewish Memory*, Schocken Books 1989, p. 105.
4 http://philosophersforchange.org/2014/07/01/anti-public -intellectuals-and-the-tyranny-of-manufactured-forgetting.
5 John Pilger, ' "Good" and "Bad" War and the Struggle of Memory Against Forgetting', *Truthout* (14 February 2014).
6 Ernest Renan in his lecture 'What is a Nation?' (1882).
7 Eric Hobsbawm, *Fractured Times: Culture and Society in the Twentieth Century*, Abacus 2014.
8 Eric Hobsbawm, 'Some Reflections on "The Break-up of Britain" ', *The New Left Review* (105) (1977).
9 Eric Hobsbawm, 'The Nation and Globalization', *Constellations* (March 1998).
10 Louis Dumont, cited in Leonidas Donskis, *The End of Ideology and Utopia? Moral Imagination and Cultural Criticism in the Twentieth Century*, Peter Lang 2000, p. 147.
11 Vytautas Kavolis, *Civilization Analysis as a Sociology of Culture*, The Edwin Mellen Press 1995, pp. 153–4.

12 Ernest Gellner, 'The Rest of History', *Prospect* (May 1996): 34–8, pp. 34–5.
13 Ibid., 36–8.
14 See Larry Wolff, *Inventing Eastern Europe: Map of Civilization on the Mind of the Enlightenment*, Stanford University Press 1994.
15 Heinrich Gotthard von Treitschke, 'Das deutsche Ordensland Preußen', *Preußische Jahrbücher* 10 (1862): 95–151.
16 Heinrich Gotthard von Treitschke, 'Unsere Aussichten', *Preußische Jahrbücher* 44 (1879): 559–76.
17 Göran Rosenberg, *La Nouvelle Lettre Internationale*, 2000.
18 Zygmunt Bauman, *Community: Seeking Safety in an Insecure World*, Polity 2001, p. 11.
19 Eric Hobsbawm, 'Enlightenment and Achievement: The Emancipation of Jewish Talent since 1800' in *Fractured Times: Culture and Society in the Twentieth Century*, Abacus 2014.
20 Eric Hobsbawm, 'Mitteleuropean Destinies' in Hobsbawm, *Fractured Times*.
21 See also Zygmunt Bauman, *Modernity and Ambivalence*, Polity 1991, p. 121.
22 See Moritz Goldstein, 'German Jewry's Dilemma', reprinted in *Leo Baeck Institute Yearbook*, 2: 236–54, pp. 237–9.
23 See Michael Burawoy, 2014 International Sociological Society presidential address: 'Facing an Unequal World'.
24 https://w2.vatican.va/content/francesco/en/apost_exhortations/documents/papa-francesco_esortazione-ap_20131124_evangelii-gaudium.html.
25 Ibid.

4: Shadows of Forgotten Ancestors? Manichaeism Revisited

1 Vytautas Kavolis, *Moralizing Cultures*, University Press of America 1993, p. 48.
2 Piotr Nowak, *Hodowanie troglodytów* ('Breeding Troglodytes'), Fundacja Augusta Hrabiego Cieszkowskiego 2014.
3 See Stanley Fish, 'Boutique Multiculturalism, or Why Liberals Are Incapable of Thinking about Hate Speech', *Critical Inquiry* 23 (2) (Winter 1997): 378–95; and *The Trouble with Principle*, Harvard University Press 1999.
4 Fish, *The Trouble with Principle*, p. 56.
5 Ibid., p. 60.
6 As his English editor Keith Gessen explains, 'Medvedev has said that what troubled him most [was] that, in the end, all of this was in some profound way irrelevant. Arguments about poetry never spilled over

into real life. They didn't change anyone's behaviour' (Kirill Medvedev, *It's No Good*, n+1 / ugly duckling presse 2012, p. 14).

7 Ibid., p. 125.
8 Ibid., p. 119.
9 Ibid., p. 130.
10 David J. Levy, ' "The Religion of Light" on Mani and Manichaeism' in Johann P. Arnason, S. N. Eisenstadt and Björn Wittrock (eds.), *Axial Civilizations and World History*, Brill 2005, pp. 319–36, pp. 335–6.
11 www.newadvent.org/cathen/09591a.htm.
12 www.newworldencyclopedia.org/entry/Manichaeism.
13 www.britannica.com/EBchecked/topic/362167/Manichaeism.
14 http://coursesa.matrix.msu.edu/~hst306/documents/indust.html.
15 www.users.cloud9.net/~bradmcc/theleme.html.
16 Ibid.
17 In William Blake, *Songs of Experience*, 1794.